GREEK AND ROMAN RELIGION

A Source Book

Greek and Roman Religion

A Source Book

by

John Ferguson

NOYES CLASSICAL STUDIES

NOYES PRESS

PARK RIDGE, NEW JERSEY

Copyright © 1980 by John Ferguson
Library of Congress Catalog Card Number: 79-23009
ISBN: 0-8155-5055-3
Printed in the United States

Published in the United States of America by
Noyes Press
Noyes Building, Park Ridge, New Jersey 07656

Library of Congress Cataloging in Publication Data

Ferguson, John, 1921–
    Greek and Roman religion.

    (Noyes classical studies)
    Bibliography: p.
    Includes indexes.
    1. Greece-–Religion. 2. Rome-–Religion.
I. Title.
BL730.F47   292   79-23009
ISBN 0-8155-5055-3

for
SONIA

Foreword

This is primarily a sourcebook of Greek and Roman religion. As such it has inevitable limitations. It depends on the written or inscribed word, and cannot take the same account of other visible remains—temples, shrines, altars, statues, reliefs, paintings—which form much of our primary evidence. Even in verbal passages there are limitations. Too long a passage may occupy a disproportionate amount of a short book; a series of short passages makes for tedious reading. Sometimes the general temper of an author tells us more than any particular passage; sometimes a gem may be incorporated in a large plain setting, but not yield up its fulness except in context. None the less in an age when fewer people read Greek and Latin in the original, and more and more take an interest in classical civilization, it is important to make available primary sources as widely as possible.

I have taught about Greek and Roman religion for many years, in three continents, at many levels, from elementary and summary introductions for nonspecialist freshmen through final honours special subject work to post-graduate seminars, and in teaching have always learned. The selection of passages arises principally from those courses. But I have trod on the shoulders of others and consulted two well-known anthologies from the Library of Greek Thought, F.M. Cornford's *Greek Religious Thought*

(London 1923) and E.R. Bevan's *Later Greek Religion* (London 1927). I have also filched unashamedly from two brilliant compilations by F.C. Grant—*Hellenistic Religions* (Indianapolis 1953) and *Ancient Roman Religion* (New York 1957). Richmond Lattimore's *Themes on Greek and Latin Epitaphs* (Urbana 1962) has proved another useful quarry. All passages have been newly translated for this volume, and defects of translation are my own, though I have of course checked other versions when available. Thanks to my wife for another of her scintillating indexes, and to the Noyes Press for their personal helpfulness and professional skill.

John Ferguson
President, Selly Oak Colleges
Formerly Dean and Director of
Studies in Arts, The Open University
United Kingdom

John Ferguson is the author of *Religions of the Roman Empire,* and in addition to teaching in British and other Universities, he has also taught in four American Universities.

TABLE OF CONTENTS

1. The Olympians

When the Hellenes, an Indo-European people, swept down in successive waves from the north, they brought with them their sky-god, Zeus or Dyaus. In Greece they encountered an established mother-goddess, who went by different names in different parts, but who was known around Argos as Hera, Our Lady. At Pylos she bore a name of similar meaning, Potnia. The settlement of the nomadic tribes with their sky-god upon the land was well expressed by the union of god and goddess: in any case the Sacred Marriage of Sky and Earth had long been celebrated as a fertility-cult in the eastern Mediterranean.

APHRODITE:
 The pure Heaven is passionate to pierce the Earth;
 passion grips the Earth to enjoy marriage.
 Rain falls from the bridegroom Heaven
 and makes Earth pregnant; she bears for mankind
 pasture for flocks and Demeter's gift of life.
 From the moisture of their marriage the trees in season
 come to full growth. In all this I share.
    Aeschylus *Danaids* fr. 44 (Athenaeus 13,600B).

In some parts, the earth-mother was known as Gaia, Ge or De. As De-meter (Mother Earth) she was strong in Arcadia. When Zeus first arrived her power predominated; he was known as

Posis Das (Earth's Consort) or Poseidon. When a new wave of Hellenes arrived they did not recognize their own god under this title and made of him Zeus' brother and gave him the sea for his domain. Poseidon is prominent as the great god of Pylos in the Mycenaean Age. The Great Goddess had other forms and identities as well. As Artemis she was Mistress of the Wild Animals with a great cult-centre across the Aegean at Ephesus; as Athene she presided over the rocky fortress at Athens, with owl and snake as her emblems; as Aphrodite, she crossed from Asia to Cyprus, "born of the foam" as her name says, showing her emergence from the sea and from the moisture surrounding the semen. Sometimes she loses her divinity, and innumerable stories of Zeus' amours with girls of all sort represent different versions of the union of peoples, and the union of sky and earth, depicted in myth.

> Majesty accords but ill with love.
> Leaving the sceptre of his power above,
> the god who wields the lightning, the great god
> who makes the universe tremble at his nod,
> puts on the likeness of a bull, and lows
> among the other cattle as he goes
> stately through the pasture, the colour of untrodden
> snow before the south wind melts it sodden.
> A dewlap hung in front, the muscles stood
> out on his neck, his horns, though slender, could
> have been an artist's work, more pure and clear
> than pearls. His brow and eyes inspired no fear,
> his face was tranquil. Europa gazed in wonder.
> So handsome! With no threat of battle under.
> But gentle as he was, she feared to meet him.
> Presently she brought some flowers to greet him.
> The lover was glad, and began to plant a kiss
> on her hands, while dreaming of his future bliss,
> scarcely restrained himself, playfully danced through the land,
> then laid his white body down on the golden sand.
> Little by little she laid aside her doubt,
> patted his chest, twined fresh flowers in and out
> of his horns, plucked up courage to settle
> herself on his back, not knowing his divine mettle.
> Gradually the god edged from the firm set turf,
> and put his borrowed feet into the surf,

went further, triumphantly carrying his prize
into the open sea. Gripping horn and back, with fearful eyes
she glanced over her shoulder at the receding coast.
Her dress fluttered and rippled in the gust.

Ovid *Metamorphoses* 2, 846-75.

As the centuries passed a canonical twelve gods were identified as holding the power on Mt. Olympus. "By the Twelve!" was a
familiar oath, and there was at Athens an altar of the Twelve, and
at Olympia six altars, each to a divine pair. The Twelve, with Zeus
always supreme, were Zeus, Hera, Poseidon, Demeter, Apollo,
Artemis, Ares, Aphrodite, Hermes, Athene, Hephaestus, Hestia.
Some of these names are found in Mycenaean texts—Zeus, Hera,
Poseidon, Artemis, Hermes, certainly; Ares, Athene, Hephaestus
possibly; Enyalios and Paian, later identified with Ares and Apollo,
possibly. There was a well-developed pantheon, but the Twelve
were not yet singled out. Apollo, in many ways the embodiment
of the Hellenic spirit, was not originally Hellenic. His two great
cult-centres, at Delphi and Delos, and his double name, Phoebus
Apollo, suggest a double origin, perhaps a northern god of the Assembly being fused with an eastern sun-god. He was an oracular
god, a god of healing, of music, of youth, of culture. Ares, perhaps
in origin a sun-god from Thrace, was to the Greeks a cruel blood-
thirsty war-god. Hermes was in origin the personification of the
cairn, which guides travellers in mountainous country; the lin-
guistic argument for this is implausible, but the functional argument strong; he naturally protected travellers and traders, became
the gods' messenger, and escorted the dead to their eternal home.
Hephaestus was perhaps in origin the power of the oil-fields with
their explosive fire. So he was associated with the power of fire, a
god of the smiths. Hestia is altogether gentler, purely Hellenic, the
goddess of the hearth. But when Dionysus, who had been known
in Mycenaean times, a god of wild nature, of intoxication and ecstatic religion, swept cataclysmically back into Greece, a place had
to be found for him on Olympus, and it was the gentle Hestia
whom he ousted, thereby destroying the balance of male and female—though he had an effeminate streak himself.

Zeus is predominant, by power.

> "Come, you gods, have a try, then you'll all know.
> Dangle a rope of gold from the sky.
> All you gods and all you goddesses take hold of it.
> You would not have the strength to pull from heaven to earth
> Zeus, who is supreme in wisdom, not for all your efforts.
> But when once I was of a mind to pull,
> then pull you up I should, earth, sea and all,
> binding the rope around the peak of Olympus
> and leaving everything suspended in mid-air.
> So far am I superior to gods and men."
>
> > Homer *Iliad* 8, 18-27.

In this predominance lay the seeds of a later monotheism or virtual monotheism.

> Zeus is to be our starting-point. We men never leave his name
> unspoken. Every street is filled with Zeus,
> every concourse of men; the sea and ports
> are filled with him. We all need Zeus at all times.
> We are his offspring.
>
> > Aratus *Phaenomena* 1-5.

> The last phrase is quoted in Acts 17:28.

Zeus' great temple was at Olympia, where his four-yearly festival was a period of truce among the Greeks. There was there a notable statue of the god by Phidias.

> Phidias is regarded as a better sculptor in the portrayal of gods
> than of men, and far above any rival in ivory work; this would be
> true even if he had produced nothing apart from his Minerva at
> Athens, and his Olympian Zeus at Elis, a statue whose glory may
> be said to have added something to revealed religion.
>
> > Quintilian 12, 10, 9.

> Minerva, i.e., Athene: this is the Athene Parthenos, known to us in
> Roman copies. Dio Chrysostom's twelfth speech contains an appre-
> ciation of Phidias' work.

But though Zeus, and in general the Olympian deities, might arouse awe they did not in general awaken feelings of love.

> It would be ridiculous for anyone to say that he loved Zeus.
> Aristotle *Magna Moralia* 1208 b 30.

Hera was surely the Earth-Mother, though some have challenged this. Her special seat was Argos, and Homer calls her "Argive Hera." Some totemistic connections there must be too, from her epithet "cow-faced." She was a goddess who looked after women at all stages.

> Tradition records that Pelasgus' son Temenus, used to live in Stymphalus, and brought up Hera. He established her three cult-titles, Maid for her girlhood, Wife for her marriage with Zeus, Widow after her quarrel with Zeus for some reason and her return to Stymphalus.
> Pausanias 8, 22, 2.

> Stymphalus is in Arcadia.

Among the most vivid pictures of gods in *The Iliad* is the portrayal of Apollo spreading destruction among the Greeks.

> He spoke in prayer, and Phoebus Apollo heard him,
> and marched down from the peaks of Olympus with anger
>   in his heart,
> carrying his bow and covered quiver on his shoulders,
> and the arrows clanged on his shoulders in his anger
> as he moved. He came like the night.
> His silver bow twanged with a chilling sound.
> He began by attacking the mules and swift hounds,
> then directed his sharp shafts against the men
> and struck home. Many pyres for the dead began to blaze.
> Homer *Iliad* 1, 43-52.

He is a god who destroys and a god who heals; he carries the bow in war and the lyre in peace. He rules at Delphi where he took over as ancient oracle of earth. He is majestically portrayed in the pediment of the great temple at Olympia.

The most attractive of the Homeric Hymns contain myths, and tend therefore to be long. The hymn to Artemis is one of the short ones.

> Muse, sing a hymn to Artemis, sister to the Far-shooting god,
> the virgin who loves arrows, and grew up with Apollo,
> who waters her horses in Meles with its thick reeds
> and speedily drives her golden chariot through Smyrna
> to vine-clad Claros, where Apollo of the silver bow
> sits waiting for the Far-shooting goddess who loves arrows.
> I greet you in song, Artemis, and all goddesses.
> But you first, you are the start of my song,
> I have sung often of you first before turning to another hymn.
>
> Homer *Hymn* 9.

The Far-shooting god: Apollo.

· Artemis had her great centre at Ephesus, where her temple became one of the wonders of the world.

One other of the Olympians must have special mention here. This is Athene, familiar from her care and support for Odysseus in *The Odyssey*, and from her association with Athens. She seems to have come in with the Hellenes as Zeus' Valkyrie daughter, and been identified with the local goddess at Athens. Like Hera she has totemic associations, as the Homeric epithet "owl-faced" and the use of the owl as her emblem suggest. But by the time of the Homeric poems she is fully personified. One of the most interesting records of the goddess comes from the town of Lindos on the island of Rhodes. The temple-chronicle of Athene Lindia contains an account of various epiphanies of the goddess. It dates from 99 B.C. The first episode is dated 490 B.C., the third 305-4 B.C. A fourth is too fragmentary to make anything of it.

When Darius, the King of Persia, sent out a great force to enslave Greece, this was the first of the islands to be visited by his naval expedition. The local inhabitants were terrified at the onset of the Persians and took refuge in all the fortified places. The majority packed themselves into Lindos. The foreigners were settling down for a siege, until the citizens of Lindos, hard pressed by shortage of water, were contemplating surrendering the city to the enemy. At that very moment the goddess stood over one of the magistrates as he slept and urged him to keep up his courage; she was going to ask her father for the water they needed. The man who received the vision reported Athene's injunctions to the citizen-body. They examined their resources and found that they had water enough for five days only. They therefore requested the Persians for a truce for that period only, saying that Athene had sent to her father for help, and if it failed to arrive within the prescribed period they agreed to surrender the city. Immediately on hearing this Darius' admiral Datis burst into laughter but the very next day a large cloud stood over the acropolis, and there was a heavy rainstorm in the centre of it, so that contrary to all probability the besieged had plenty of water and the Persian forces went short. The foreigner was profoundly shaken by the goddess's epiphany. He divested himself of the decorations he was wearing and made an offering of them—his cloak, necklace and armbands, and his diadem and scimitar as well, and even his chariot. This last was formerly preserved here, but during the priesthood of Halius Eucles, Astyanactidas' son, it was destroyed in a conflagration of the temple along with the majority of the dedications. Datis broke camp and went about his business, but not without contracting an agreement with the besieged and declaring publicly "These men are under the gods' protection". . . .

When Halios Pythanna, Archipolis' son, held the office of priest in Lindos, a man managed to get himself locked in the temple at night without anyone's knowledge, and hanged himself from the beams attached to the wall at the back of the cult-statue. The citizens of Lindos were on the point of taking the decision to send to Delphi and inquire what ought to be done about the occurrence when the goddess stood over the priest while he was lying asleep and told him to rest easy as far as she was concerned, but to strip part of the roof immediately above the statue, and leave it so till three suns had passed and the place was purified by water sent from her father; then they were to replace the roof as it was before, purify the temple with the accustomed rites and offer the traditional sacrifices to Zeus. . . .

When the city was under siege from Demetrius, Callicles, who had retired from the priesthood of Athene Lindia but was still living in Lindos, thought the goddess stood over him in his sleep and instructed him to take a message to one of the senior magistrates named Anaxapolis, advising him to write to King Ptolemy and invite him to come to the city's rescue, as the goddess herself would take command and secure victory and power. If he failed to take the message to the magistrate, or if the latter failed to write to Ptolemy, it would be the worse for him. On the first occasion of seeing the vision Callicles kept quiet, but the same thing occurred several times—on six consecutive nights the goddess stood over him with the same instructions; so Callicles went to the city, told his tale to the members of the Council and opened the matter to Anaxapolis. The members of the Council sent Anaxapolis to Ptolemy.

Lindos: *Fouilles et Recherches 1902-14:* II Inscriptions No. 2.

From early times the Romans were influenced by the Greek culture established round the bay of Naples, and it was not long before they brought their pantheon into conformity with the Greek pantheon. Some of the gods were already there. Jupiter, Dyaus-piter, is recognizable as Father Zeus; Apollo, an Etruscan god, is unchanged; Vesta is identical with Hestia. Others required more ingenious adaptation. Juno, the power of feminine fertility, corresponding to the male Genius, was identified with Hera. Neptunus, a spirit of water, became Poseidon. Ceres, a power of the growing crops (compare *creare*), was one with Demeter. Artemis became Diana, also a spirit of the wildwood; her opposite number Dianus or Janus, an oak-god, who came into the city with the solid oak gates and became a door-god, looking both ways, a god of opening and closing, was not one of the Twelve but retained his importance. Mars, whose field was agriculture as well as war, became increasingly isolated in the latter as a result of his fusion with Ares. Aphrodite had her equivalent in a garden-spirit called Venus. Hermes found his in the spirit of trading-gain, Mercurius. Athene was equated with an Etruscan goddess of technical skill, Minerva. Hephaestus found a natural double in Volcanus, the very personification of volcanic fire. We might also mention Saturnus, perhaps originally a spirit of sowing, who found a Greek identity in Cronos, the father of Zeus.

It will be noted that many of the Roman deities are spirits associated with a particular object or limited function. Such spirits are not the stuff of which myths are made, and nearly all the divine myths are taken over from the Greek, though the Romans had their own heroic legends. Indeed some of the Roman divinities are barely personified. Venus, like *onus* or *corpus*, is neuter in form, and the shepherds' god Pales is indifferently masculine or feminine. A common Roman formula for prayer is, "whether you be a god or goddess."

One other aspect of the Olympian religion must be noted. As the believers in the Olympian gods spread into other parts of the world they found gods with different names, and often tried to find an identification in their own pantheon. This was particularly true of the Romans: it is sometimes called the "Roman interpretation." Mars, the soldiers' god, in particular, acquired a bewildering variety of sub-identities. The whole process can be exemplified by two dedications from Britain.

> To the God Mars Medocius of the Lowlanders and to the Victory of our Emperor Alexander the Saintly and Blessed, Lossio Veda, a Caledonian of the clan of Vepogenus, offered this gift out of his own purse.
>
> *The Roman Inscriptions of Britain* 191.
>
> From Colchester. The spelling of the original is somewhat phonetic.
>
> To Rigocalatis, Toutatis, and Mars Cocidius as a result of a vow Vitalis made this offering.
>
> *The Roman Inscriptions of Britain* 1017.
>
> In Lowther Castle from some site in Cumberland. The name of Mars seems intrusive among the Celtic gods. Rigocalatis and Toutatis are widespread. Cocidius is a local god.

We must now return to the Homeric poems, influential as they were in shaping the thought of the later Greeks, and consider the general view of life they offer. The Olympian religion in Homer is not without a moral element. For example, the Homeric gods are protectors of justice.

> The blessed gods do not welcome actions of violence,
> but reward justice and virtuous actions from men.
>
> Homer Odyssey 14, 83-4.

Again, strangers are under the special protection of Zeus.

> Antinous, you did not do well in striking the traveller.
> Abominable man, what if he turned out some god from the sky?
> Yes, the gods put on the likeness of alien guests,
> appearing in all sorts of guises, and visiting cities,
> to inspect men's unjust or righteous behaviour.
>
> Homer Odyssey 17, 483-91.

One of the most sinister conceptions is that of Ate or Doom. Here Agamemnon is explaining that his folly was not of his own volition.

> I was not to blame.
> Zeus, Fate and the Fury who walks in the dark,
> placed a savage doom on my mind at the assembly
> on the day when I took the decision to confiscate
>   Achilles' award.
> But what could I do? A god has all in her hands,
> Zeus' eldest daughter Doom, who dooms us all
> in her malice. She moves lightly, never touching
> the ground, but enters men's heads,
> and corrupts them, bringing one or another to the ground.
> She even played her doom-tricks on Zeus. . . .
>
> Homer Iliad 19, 86-95.

Fate, or Moira, is in general the instrument of Zeus. But sometimes Fate is independent of Zeus, and he would defy her at his peril.

> When the son of cunning Cronos saw them he was sad,
> and spoke to his wife and sister Hera:

"Oh! Fate has decreed that my beloved Sarpedon
must fall before Menoetius' son Patroclus.
My heart is being torn in two as I think about it.
Should I snatch him out of the sorrows of battle
and set him down alive in the rich country of Lycia,
or should I now crush him at Patroclus' hands?"
Then lady Hera with the ox-eyes answered:
"Son of Cronos, your majesty, what a thing to say!
Do you really intend to rescue from death's grim clangour
a mortal, long destined to doom by Fate?
Do so. But all the rest of us gods will not approve."
Homer Iliad 16, 431-43.

So Pindar says (*Paean* 6, 94) that "Zeus, overseer of the gods, dared not relax what was fated." In general we may say that the divine powers are held responsible for man's lot, and the picture of that lot is pessimistic. Achilles puts this vividly to Priam at the end of *The Iliad*.

The gods have woven a life of misery,
carefree themselves, into our mortal lot.
Two jars stand on the floor of Zeus' palace,
full of his gifts, one of curses, one of blessings.
Zeus the Thunderer gives some a mixed dowry;
they encounter disaster at one minute, success at the next.
But when he gives a man from the jar of sorrows, he makes him
    an outcast,
deprivation pursues him over the lovely face of the earth,
he wanders condemned by gods and by men.
Homer Iliad 24, 525-33.

But in the later of the two great Homeric poems, *The Odyssey*, Zeus puts the responsibility back squarely on man's own shoulders.

Oh, what accusations mortals bring against the gods!
From us, they claim that evil comes, but themselves
through their own headstrong behaviour receive evils beyond
    their destiny.
Aegisthus for example, who went beyond his destiny and lay with
Agamemnon's wedded wife—and killed him on his return,

though he knew of the sheer destruction, since we warned him
    beforehand,
sending Hermes, the keen-sighted killer of Argus,
not to kill Agamemnon or court his wife;
for vengeance for Agamemnon would arise from Orestes,
once he came of age, and began to long for his own land.
So Hermes said, but his kindly intentions did not sway
Aegisthus's intentions—and now he has paid in full for all his
    crimes.

Homer Odyssey 1, 33-43.

This pessimistic view is inherited by other writers. Here is
Semonides (seventh century B.C.).

My son, Zeus the Thunderer holds the destiny
of all things and disposes them by his will.
There's no understanding in man: creatures of a day,
we live like cattle, and do not know
how God shall bring each of us to his destined end.
But Hope and Confidence keep us going,
our minds on the unattainable; some await
the coming of a single day, others the cycle of years.
Next year, every mortal imagines he'll return
feathered with riches and possessions.
But unenvied age seizes one
before he reaches port; another's heart
is worn with illness; another is overpowered by Ares
and sent by Hades below the black earth.
Some at sea are wrecked by storms
and wave upon wave of the dark ocean
and lose their lives, when they've loaded the ship with livelihood.
Others tie a noose around their wretched necks
and leave the sunlight by their own choice.
Nothing is free from evil. Ten thousand
dooms assail us humans, our anxieties and sorrows
are beyond imagination. If anyone would listen to me,
we should not set our hearts on good things, or torture
ourselves by fixing our minds on disasters.

Semonides fr. 1.

Here, in the following century, is Theognis of Megara.

Cyrnus, no-one is responsible for his own profit and disaster,
    the gods grant both;
no-one as he works knows within him whether he's moving
    to failure or success.
Often when he thinks things will turn out badly they turn out well,
    when well, badly.
All a man wishes never comes his way;
    it contains grim uncertainty.
In our ignorance we men practise idle actions.
    The gods will and fulfil all.

                               Theognis 133-42.

Here is the same note of pessimism in Sophocles.

Zeus, how can man's
presumption check your power?
It is not subject to sleep which makes all else old
or to the gods' tireless
months. Ageless, everlasting monarch,
you live in Olympus'
marble splendour.
Now and in time to come,
as in the past, this law
is all: nothing passes
into man's life with glory, without disaster.

                                  Sophocles *Antigone* 604-14.

It echoes down the ages and appears, turned to a more constructive end in conjunction with the Epicurean view that necessity is the mother of invention, in the gentle spirit of Vergil.

        The Father did not wish
the path of agriculture to be smooth; he was the first to turn
the fields by science, sharpening men's wits with troubles,
not letting his realms slumber in heavy sloth.

                               Vergil *Georgics* 1, 121-4.

We may close this sketch of Olympian religion with a satire from the second century A.D. Lucian of Samosata was influenced by the Epicureans to poke fun at traditional religion. Plainly there would be no satire were he not exaggerating the picture of the life of the Olympians held by many people in his own day.

> When I had answered all these questions Zeus said: "Menippus, tell me what mankind thinks of me." "Your majesty," I replied, "in the most pious way of course, as king of all the gods." "Have fun," he said, "I'm perfectly well aware of their craze for novelty; no need for you to tell me. There was once a time when they thought of me as a seer and doctor; I was all in all to them.
>
> Every street is filled with Zeus,
> every concourse of men.
>
> In those days Dodona and Pisa were glorious, cynosures. I couldn't even see for the smoke of sacrifices. But once Apollo established his oracle at Delphi, Asclepius his hospital at Pergamum, once the temples sprang up to Bendis in Thrace and Anubis in Egypt and Artemis in Ephesus, that's where they all flock, that's where they celebrate festivals, that's where they sacrifice hecatombs and offer bars of gold. I'm regarded as passé; they think they've done me enough honour by sacrificing once every four years at Olympia. You can see for yourself: my altars are cold and bare, worse than Plato's Laws or Chrysippus' Syllogisms."
>
> In the course of this discussion we arrived at the place where he had to sit and listen to prayers. There was a row of apertures, rather like wellheads, with covers on them, and a golden throne alongside each. Zeus sat down by the first, took off the cover, and lent attention to the prayers of the people—a mixed bag from all over the world. I stood alongside him, leant over and listened to the prayers with him. They ran like this: "O Zeus, grant me to become a king!" "O Zeus, grant that my onions and garlic may sprout!" "O gods, grant that my father may have a speedy death!" One of them would say: "Grant that I may inherit my wife's estate!" "Grant that my plot against my brother may go undetected!" "Grant that I may win my suit!" "Grant that I may be a victor at Olympia!" One sailor would be praying for the north wind to blow, another for the south; a farmer would be praying for rain, a laundryman for a fine day. Zeus listened and examined each prayer carefully, but made no extravagant promises:
>
> Some things the Father granted, others refused.
>
> He hoisted up the just prayers through the mouth of the aperture, and transferred them to his right; he dismissed the unrighteous

prayers ungranted, with a blast of air to take them down as far away from heaven as possible. There was one prayer over which I observed him in a complete quandary. Two men were making diametrically opposed requests with the promise of equal sacrifices, and he had no means of deciding which to support. He reached a state of Academic suspension, incapable of coming to a verdict. Just like Pyrrho, he suspended judgement and left it an open question.

When he had given adequate attention to the prayers he moved to the next throne and the second aperture, stooped over and concentrated on oaths and contracts. He dealt with these, crushing Hermodorus the Epicurean, and moved his seat to the next throne to attend to omens (sounds, words and auguries). Next he transferred to the sacrifice aperture; the rising smoke reported to Zeus the name of each of the sacrificers. When he had finished with all these he gave the winds and weather their orders: "Rain today in Scythia, a thunderstorm in Libya, snow in Greece. North Wind, Lydia for you. South Wind, a holiday. West Wind, a storm on the Adriatic and a ton of hail all over Cappadocia."

By now he'd more or less settled everything, and we went off to the dining-room, as it was dinner-time. Hermes took charge of me and gave me a place alongside Pan, the Corybants, Attis and Sabazios (immigrant gods of uncertain standing). Demeter provided me with bread, Dionysus with wine, Heracles with meat, Aphrodite with scent, and Poseidon with whitebait. I managed to get some surreptitious sips of ambrosia and nectar. That nice Ganymede was kind to me: whenever he noticed Zeus looking the other way, he ran the risk of bringing me a spoonful or two of nectar. The gods don't eat bread or "drink the ruby wine," as Homer puts it (he must have been there and seen with his own eyes like me). Their main dish is ambrosia, and they get drunk on nectar. They greatly enjoy dining on the smoke from sacrifices, which comes up impregnated with all the savours, and the blood of the victims, which the sacrificers let stream over the altars.

During the meal Apollo played the lute, Silenus danced sexily, the Muses rose to their feet and sang a section of Hesiod's *Theogony* and the first song from Pindar's *Hymns*. When we'd all had enough we went to sleep as we were where we were, fairly sozzled.

The rest, gods and cavalry officers,
slept through the night, but sleep could not hold me.

I was meditating on a lot of questions: for example how had Apollo never grown a beard in all that time, and how can night come in Heaven when the Sun is always there and sharing in the fun.

Lucian *Icaromenippus* 24-8.

Lucian pictures Menippus (a Hellenistic philosopher) flying up to heaven. But he is an Icarus not a Daedalus: the implication is that he didn't really find the true heaven. The first quotation comes from the Aratus passage already quoted. Dodona: the temple and oracle of Zeus in Epirus. Pisa: the district round Olympia. Bendis: a Thracian goddess, whose worship was established in Piraeus in the fifth century B.C. Anubis: jackal-headed Egyptian god. Chrysippus (c. 280-207 B.C.): third head of the Stoic school. Pyrrho (c. 360-270 B.C.): Sceptical philosopher, who denied the possibility of certainty, and advocated suspension of judgement. Corybants: ecstatic worshippers of Cybele, the Mother-goddess of Asia Minor. Attis: consort of Cybele, the young god who dies. Sabazios: god from Phrygia, regarded by the Greeks as alien, but identified with Dionysus. The other quotations are from Homer.

2. The Religion of the Countryside

The countryside was the realm of the divine. Every part was instinct with divine life. Above was the holy sky, not always visible in the city's narrow streets; below was the sacred soil of the Earth-Mother, paved and remote in the city. Every bush had its Dryad, every stream its Naiad. There is an illuminating note in Servius, the commentator on Vergil.

> HAMADRYADS: nymphs who are born with trees and die with them, like the one whom Erysichthon killed. He laid an axe to a tree, and a voice rang out and blood spurted, as Ovid tells us. Dryads are nymphs living in trees, Oreads in mountains. Perimelids are nymphs who take their name from sheep, Naiads from rivers, Limonids from meadows, and Curotrophae from the nursing of infants.
>
> Servius on Vergil *Eclogues* 10, 62.

The names are derived from the Greek.

- Round any corner you might encounter goatfoot Pan, the god of all Nature. Some animals were sacred to and no doubt originally manifestations of divine powers, and there were other divinities—Artemis, say, or Cybele, or Dionysus—who came to exercise a wider sway over nature in the raw. Hermes was there in the stones which marked the way. Mountains were the meeting-place of

17

heaven and earth, and sacred, numinous spots. No one would venture to their tops except for religious devotion, unless out of military necessity. We have lost this: any African will understand it. Here is Strabo's description of the tract of country at the mouth of the river Alpheus.

> The whole area is full of shrines to Artemis, or Aphrodite, or the Nymphs, in precincts which, because of the abundance of water, are generally carpeted with flowers. There are numerous herms along the roads, and shrines of Poseidon on the headlands by the coast.
>
> Strabo 8, 3, 12 (343).

Aelian's description of the celebrated Vale of Tempe is not dissimilar; he passes from the greenness and coolness to the shrines and sacrifices.

> Next for a full verbal picture of the place in Thessaly known as Tempe. The account, provided it is well presented, has all the interest of the descriptions of works by artistic geniuses, as everyone will agree. It is a place situated between Olympus and Ossa. These are very high mountains, pulled apart by some divine providence, leaving a space in between extending to a length of five miles, and a hundred feet wide or in parts slightly more. The river Peneius flows through the middle. The other rivers form confluents with it, and add their water to it, making the Peneius quite sizeable. This valley offers all sorts of places to stop, not of human construction, but formed by nature's spontaneous ambition for beauty at the point when the place was created. Ivy grows and flourishes, streaming in rich profusion and climbing up the tall trees and growing with them just like the best vines. Quantities of convolvulus actually climb the crag and give shade to the rock. In fact the rock lies out of sight underneath. There is nothing to be seen but vegetation; it is a regular festival for the eyes. In the level, low-lying ground there are coppices of great variety with rides running right through them, marvellous retreats for travellers in the height of summer, providing, as they do, a welcome coolness. They are pierced by plenty of streams, with pools of delicious cool water. This water is said to be excellent to bathe in and conducive to health. Birds of all sorts, song-birds especially, are making music all around; it is a feast for the ears as they provide a gentle,

kindly escort and banish the travelers' weariness with their singing.

On either bank of the river are the places to stop and rest I mentioned before. The river Peneius passes through the middle of Tempe with an easy, leisurely flow like that of oil. There is plenty of shade on the river from the trees on the banks and their overhanging boughs, and for most of the day this extends to keep off the sun and enable those in boats to travel in coolness. The people round about live in harmony with one another, and join in sacrifice, get-togethers, wine-parties. There are so many people offering sacrifice all the time that, as you would expect, the most delicious savours accompany those who pass by in boats or on foot. Lasting religious honour has conferred holiness on the place where the children of Thessaly say that Pythian Apollo was purified in accordance with Zeus' orders after killing the snake Pytho, the guardian of Delphi, at the time when the Earth-goddess was still responsible for the oracle. They say that he, son of Zeus and Leto, garlanded himself from this laurel-tree in Tempe and took a branch in his right hand, and so came to Delphi and took over the oracle. There is an altar at the very point where he put on the garland and plucked the branch. Even today every ninth year the noble families of Delphi send a procession of their children with one of their own number as Leader of the Sacred Embassy. They arrive and offer splendid sacrifices in Tempe and leave with garlands plaited from the very tree from which the god plaited his garland on that occasion. The road they take is called the Pythian road. It runs through Thessaly, Pelasgia, Oeta, the territory of the Aenianes, of the Malians, Doris and Western Locris. There people all escort the procession with great ceremony and respect, just like those who do honour to the embassy of the Hyperboreans bringing holy offerings for the selfsame god. And they present garlands from this laurel-tree to the victors in the Pythian Games. That will have to do for an account from me of Tempe in Thessaly.

Aelian Miscellaneous Investigations 3, 1.

In Plato's *Phaedrus*, Socrates and Phaedrus stop by the river Ilissus, and Socrates speaks.

By Hera, what a glorious retreat! The plane-tree is tall and spreading, the height and shade of the agnus castus are absolutely glorious. It's in full bloom; there's a lovely fragrance about the place. What a welcome spring gushing from under the plane-tree—very

cold water too to the feel of my foot. From the figurines and statues
I would guess it was a shrine of Achelous and some of the Nymphs.
                                        Plato *Phaedrus* 230 B.

> The passage is often taken as a description of natural beauty. But, in a
> Wordsworthian sense, it is not. The points made (they go on with a
> breeze and soft grass) relate to convenience (shade, pleasant smells
> and cool water) and sanctity.

Here, similarly, is a Roman poet's view of a spring.

> Spring of Bandusia, brighter than crystal,
> worthy of rich wine, worthy of flowers,
>   tomorrow brings you a goat,
>   on whose forehead the young horns
> grow with promise of love and battles.
> It's not to be: your cool waters
>   will flow red with the blood
>   of the playful kid.
> The cruel season of blazing Sirius
> cannot touch you; you offer welcome
>   coolness to wandering herds
>   and bullocks tired with ploughing.
> You'll join the company of famous springs
> when I tell of the oak growing over the hollow
>   rocks where your chattering
>   streams leap down.
>   Horace *Odes* 3,13.

Here again is the younger Pliny describing the source of the
river Clitumnus.

> The banks are thickly clothed with ash and poplar, reflected greenly
> in the clear river which adopts them as if they were actually in the
> water. The water could rival snow for its chill—and its whiteness.
> Nearby is a holy temple of great antiquity with Clitumnus himself
> standing there wearing a robe with purple fringe. The oracular lots
> around testify that his divinity is present and has the power of
> prophecy. There are a large number of other shrines scattered
> around, each for a different god, each of whom has his own title,
> his own ceremonies, and very likely his own spring in addition.
>   Pliny *Letters* 8, 8.

— Caves were sacred places.

After Zoroaster the practice held with the rest also of performing initiatory rites in caves and grottoes, either natural or artificial. They built temples, shrines and altars to the Olympian gods, sacrificial hearths to demigods and gods of the earth, pits and trenches to gods of the underworld—and caves and grottoes to the Cosmos— and to the nymphs too, because of the waters which flow from above or below in caves; the Naiads, as I shall explain in a moment, are particularly responsible for these waters. So, as I have said, they made the cave a symbol of the Cosmos—that is the material, sensible world; in addition they took it as a symbol of all invisible powers: caves are dark, and the essence of these powers similarly obscure. So Cronos prepares a cave for himself in Ocean and there conceals his children. So too Demeter brings up the Maiden in a cave with the help of nymphs. Anyone who goes through the works of writers on religion will come on many similar examples. The dedication of caves to nymphs, particularly Naiads (whose sphere is in the springs, and who receive their name from the sources of rivers), is clear from the hymn to Apollo:

> For you the nymphs who live in the caves of the earth,
> inspired by the breath of the Muses
> to prophetic utterance, have carved out
> springs of the waters of wisdom. These cover the earth,
> burst through every river,
> provide an endless flow of fresh water
> for mankind. . . .

So before they even thought of temples, our ancestors dedicated caves and grottoes to the gods. In Crete the cave of the Curetes is dedicated to Zeus, in Arcadia there is a cave to Selene and Lycean Pan, on Naxos one to Dionysus. Everywhere Mithras was known he was propitiated by a cave. In describing the cave on Ithaca Homer was not satisfied with speaking of its two entrances, but adds that one faced north, the other south and that the northern one sloped down. He does not specify whether the southern one also sloped down, only that

> . . . men
> do not enter by it, the gods walk that way.

Porphyry *On the Cave of the Nymphs in the Odyssey* 6-8, 20.

A late philosophical treatment, but sufficient to show that at all times caves were haunts of the numinous. By the Cosmos Porphyry means Nature, considered as an ordered system. Zoroaster: the founder of

Persian religion. Cronos: father of Zeus, ousted by his son. The
hymn is in Bergk *Poetae Lyrici Graeci* 3 p 684; the Homeric quotation
from *Odyssey* 13, 111-2.

Mountains too were sacred. Apollonius and Damis in Philo-
stratus' semi-fiction are climbing through the Caucasus. Damis is
speaking.

> "Yesterday we were passing through human habitations. Today
> we are climbing divine untrodden ground. You heard our guide
> say that the natives believe this to be the home of the gods."
>
> Philostratus *Life of Apollonius of Tyana* 2, 5.

High on the great St. Bernard pass a number of bronze tablets
were found honouring the local mountain god.

> To Poeninus, for his journey and return C. Julius
> Primus gladly pays his vow as due.
>
> H. Dessau *Inscriptiones Latinae Selectae* 4850a.

Zeus often claimed the mountain-tops. A quite revealing inscription is to be read in mosaic on the top of Mt. Cynthus, the
low hill which crests Delos.

> To Zeus Cynthius and Athene Cynthia Apollonides Theogeiton's
> son from Laodicea dedicated the *kataklyston* when Aristomachus
> was priest, Nicephorus acolyte, during the administration of
> Quintus of Azenia.
>
> P. Bruneau and J. Ducat *Guide de Délos* p 150.

> *Kataklyston* is not found elsewhere and its meaning is unknown. The
> familiar divinities take on a special culture for this place.

It would be possible to expand such evidence almost indefinitely.

On the edges of the Roman world the story was the same.

There was a grove, from time immemorial never desecrated,
whose interlacing boughs banished the sunlight
and shut in a world of darkness and dull shadow.
No country Pan, no forest-lord
Silvanus, no Nymph haunted it, but savage rites
were celebrated, altars heaped with ghastly gifts,
every tree aspersed with human blood.
If past generations, who honoured the gods, merit credence,
the very birds feared to perch on the branch,
the beasts to lie down in the thickets. No breath of wind
touched those woods, no lightning struck from black
clouds. There was no breeze to stir the leaves,
but the trees trembled by themselves. Cascades of water
streamed from dark springs. The images of the gods were
grim, inartistic, shapeless, formed from lopped logs.
The mustiness, the lack of pallor, the rotting timbers
struck chill to the heart. Gods worshipped in familiar
forms are not so awesome. Not to know the gods
we dread adds to our fears. Rumour had it
that often the earth quaked, and its deep hollows boomed,
yew-trees toppled and rose up again,
flames blazed up though the trees were not on fire,
snakes glided about and turned round the trunks.
The tribes never came in numbers to worship at close quarters;
they left it to the gods. When the Sun is at high noon
or when black night grips the sky, the very priest fears
their arrival, and is scared to come on the Lord of the grove.

Lucan, 3, 399-425.

We are thus left with a sense of the numinous quality of the whole of Nature which was not remotely controlled by some with-drawn creator-god but the home and sphere of vast numbers of somewhat indeterminate spiritual beings.

In Rome the oldest strands of religion incorporated a belief not in anthropomorphic deities of the kind we usually recognize but in *numina*, divine powers of a limited function, whom German scholars called *Sondergötter* or *Augenblickgötter* (gods of the twinkling of an eye). In origin they had no existence except in relation to the function over which they presided. These functions were mainly to do with farming and family life, and it was in these two fields the *numina* particularly proliferated.

> As I said earlier, it is clear that the divine powers receive their names from their functions; for example, the god Occator receives his name from harrowing, Sarritor from hoeing, Sterculinius from dunging, Sator from sowing. Fabius Pictor lists the following gods invoked by the Priest of Ceres in sacrificing to Earth and Ceres: Vervactor, Redarator, Inporcitor, Insitor, Obarator, Occator, Sarritor, Subruncinator, Messor, Convector, Conditor, Promitor.
>
> Servius on Vergil *Georgics* 1,21.

> These are good examples of the *numina* or divine powers (the word means "nodding": it is neuter in form). The evidence is early, not antiquarian, as Fabius Pictor was writing in the third century B.C. Vervactor is associated with the first ploughing of fallow ground, Redarator with the second ploughing, Imporcitor with furrowing, Insitor with grafting, Obarator with ploughing up, Subruncinator with weeding, Messor with reaping, Convector with binding, Conditor with garnering and Promitor with the production of the food from store. These are indeed *Sondergötter*, gods of a limited function.

Christian writers like Augustine, who had an axe to grind, write scornfully about these godlings, who naturally covered the operations of home and family life as well as of farm and field. In the following passage Augustine is arguing against pagan intellectuals who claim that all the gods are different manifestations of Jupiter. We can incidentally see something of the process whereby fullscale gods emerged out of the *numina*.

> Let him be Jupiter in the aether, and Juno in the air, and Neptune in the sea, and Salacia in the lower regions of the sea, Pluto within the earth, Proserpina within the lower regions of the earth, Vesta in domestic fireplaces, Vulcan in blacksmiths' forges, sun, moon and stars among the heavenly bodies, Apollo among fortune-tellers, Mercury in business activities, in Janus let him initiate, in Terminus bring to a close, let him be Saturn in time, Mars and Bellona in war, Liber in the vineyards, Ceres among the crops, Diana in the forests, Minerva in intellectual activities.

> Finally, let him also be found in that mob of what I might call popular gods. Let him under the name of Liber supervise male seed and under the name of Libra female seed. Let him be Diespater

in bringing the product of childbirth into the light of day (*dies*). Let him be the goddess Mena who has been put in charge of women's monthly periods; let him be Lucina whom they call upon in childbirth. Let him bring help (*opem*) to newly born children by receiving them in the bosom of earth, and let him have the name Ops in that capacity. Let him open the child's mouth in a wailing cry (*vagitus*) and have the name of the god Vagitanus. Let him raise (*levet*) the child up from the ground, and have the name of the goddess Levana. Let him protect the cradle (*cunas*) and have the name of the goddess Cunina. Let no-one but he be found in those goddesses who chant the destinies of children at birth and are called Carmentes. Let him superintend chance occurrences and be known as Fortuna. As the goddess Rumina let him squeeze from the mother's breast the baby's milk (*ruma* is an archaic word for "breast"). As the goddess Potina let him serve drink (*potio*), as the goddess Educa provide food (*esca*). Let him be pronounced Paventa because of the infants' fear (*pavor*), Venitia from the emergence (*venit*) of hope, Volupia from pleasure (*voluptas*), Agenona from action (*actu*). Let him receive the name of the goddess Stimula from the goads (*stimulis*) which drive a man to excess in action, of the goddess Strenua from inducing strength, of Numeria from instruction in mathematics (*numerare*), of Camena from instruction in singing (*canere*). Let him also be the god Consus from offering counsel and the goddess Sentia from the sentiments she inspires. Let him be the goddess Iuventas for taking over the initial stages of youth at the end of adolescence, and Fortuna Barbata for putting a beard (*barba*) on their faces once they are grown up. (They had no intention of flattering the young men by turning this deity, whatever it may be, into a male god Barbatus, named after the beard, as Nodutus is named after knots (*nodi*), still less of using the male form Fortunius instead of the female Fortuna in view of the possession of a beard.) As the god Iugatinus let him join together (*iungo*) married couples, and when the virgin unfastens her belt and becomes a wife let him again be invoked as the goddess Virginensis. Let him be Mutunus or Tutunus, whom the Greeks call Priapus. If that does not make them ashamed, let him be all that I have said and more that I have not said (I did not think it right to tell the whole story). Let all these gods and goddesses be Jupiter and nothing but Jupiter—or let them all be (as some hold) parts of him or aspects of his power—the view held by learned men of great distinction who believe he is the world-soul.

Granted all this (and I do not propose to argue that point at present) what would they lose by worshipping a single god? It would certainly be cheaper!

Augustine The City of God 4,11.

Augustine's source for this is Varro. Most of the godlings speak for
themselves. Mutunus Tutunus had some part in the wedding ceremony as a phallus.

We thus have a picture of Roman religion in its origins by no
means concerned with high gods, but with the propitiation of immense numbers of divine powers concerned with the operations
and activities which really matter to life. Such a religion may be
accounted by a more sophisticated generation 'superstitious', but
it cannot be called irrelevant. To the Roman, religion is life.

We have the record of a very early ritual for the protection of
the crops.

Then the priests closed the doors, girded up their robes, took up
their missals and danced the holy three-step marking the rhythm
with the following chant:

Lases, help us,
Lases, help us,
Lases, help us!
Marmar, let no plague or ruin come upon our plenty
Marmar, let no plague or ruin come upon our plenty
Marmar, let no plague or ruin come upon our plenty!
Fierce Mars, be filled, leap high in our gateway,
                                        stand firm, wild one
Fierce Mars, be filled, leap high in our gateway,
                                        stand firm, wild one
Fierce Mars, be filled, leap high in our gateway,
                                        stand firm, wild one!
Each will call on the Gods of Sowing
                                antiphonally
Each will call on the Gods of Sowing
                                antiphonally
Each will call on the Gods of Sowing
                                antiphonally!
Marmor, help us
Marmor, help us
Marmor, help us!
Glory Glory Glory Glory Glory!

After the dance the signal was given for the public slaves to enter and they collected up the missals.

Carmen Fratrum Arvalium: H. Dessau
Inscriptiones Latinae Selectae 5039.

This is from a record of A.D. 218 but the antique formula goes back to at least the sixth century B.C. The Lares or Lases are the household gods, perhaps originally ancestral gods protecting the land around the farmstead. Mars—Marmar and Marmor are reduplicated forms of the same name—is a god of agriculture protecting the crops. He is fierce, the embryonic god of war who resists attacks, but he is also "filled." Perhaps he was in origin a *numen* of the storm. The high leap, and the dance of the priests, may be "sympathetic magic" to make the crops grow high, as the Curetes in Crete would leap for tall crops and fleecy flocks.

It is interesting to put alongside the Roman evidence an extract from the records of a priesthood at Iguvium (Gubbio) called the Atiedian Brothers, twelve in number like the *Fratres Arvales*. The gods they honour include Jupiter and Mars. Here is a private ritual of sacrifice to Jupiter Sancius on behalf of a private family.

When you intend to immolate a votive bull-calf, dedicate it to Jupiter on that very day. When you dedicate it, hold in your hand a solar ring. Make the following declaration: "Jupiter Sancius, I dedicate this votive bull-calf to you." Three times designate it in a fit state for offering; three times proclaim it a votive offering. Sacrifice it to Jupiter in the midst of the Atiedian Brothers for the clan Vucia. When you are sacrificing, wear a stole on your right shoulder. When you have completed the sacrifice lay the stole on the flat-cake. When you are making the offering wear the stole on your right shoulder. Present fruits of the field and make an offering with mead.

J.W. Poultney *The Bronze Tables of Iguvium* II b 21-9.

I have broadly followed Poultney's interpretation of the Umbrian. Jupiter Sancius is a god of oaths; the solar ring indicates the all-seeing eyes of the sun. The clan name, which may be the equivalent of the Latin Lucia, is no doubt generalized and the particular clan would be substituted, rather as Roman formulas for devoting an enemy speak of Carthage. The movement of the stole plainly marks three important stages of the sacrifice. The whole is difficult to date, but probably not later than the third century B.C.

To return to Rome: M. Porcius Cato, the "Censor" (234–149 B.C.)
wrote a treatise on agriculture which is full of the religious life of
the farm.

> When the pear is flowering make your offering for the oxen. . . .
> The offering should be made as follows. Present Jupiter of the Of-
> fering with a beaker of wine of any size you like. The day is to be a
> holiday for oxen, drivers and those making the offering. The for-
> mula for the offering runs "Jupiter of the Offering, in that it is meet
> for a beaker of wine to be offered to you in my house before my
> people, so receive our worship in the presentation of this offer-
> ing." Next the hands are to be washed and the wine lifted up with
> the words "Jupiter of the Offering, receive our worship in the
> presentation of this offering, receive our worship in this sacrificial
> wine." Bring a gift for Vesta if you wish. The offering for Jupiter
> comprises roast meat and a stoup of wine. Consecrate it to Jupiter
> devoutly approaching him in the appropriate manner. After-
> wards, when the offering is completed, plant millet, panic-grass,
> garlic, and lentils. . . .
>
> Before harvesting you should sacrifice the pre-harvest pig ac-
> cording to the following rite. Ceres should receive a sow as the
> pre-harvest pig before you garner the following crops: spelt,
> wheat, barley, beans, rape-seed. Before you sacrifice the sow offer
> a prayer accompanied by incense and a libation of wine, to Janus,
> Jupiter and Juno. Bring forward a plate of cakes for Janus with
> these words: "Father Janus, in bringing forward this plate of
> cakes I ask in all faith that you will look with kindly grace on me
> and my children, my home and household." Present the oblation-
> cake to Jupiter with these words: "Jupiter, in bringing forward this
> oblation-cake I ask in all faith that you will accept this oblation and
> look with kindly grace on me and my children, my home and
> household." Next present the wine to Janus with these words:
> "Father Janus, just as in bringing forward the plate of cakes I asked
> in all faith for your favour, so to the same end accept this sacrificial
> wine." Next address Jupiter with these words: "Jupiter, accept
> this oblation-cake and accept this sacrificial wine." Next sacrifice
> the pre-harvest pig. When the entrails have been cut out, bring
> forward a plate of cakes for Janus and offer it with the same ritual
> as you used previously. Bring forward an oblation-cake for Jupiter
> and offer it with the same ritual as you used previously. In the
> same manner, offer wine to Janus and offer wine to Jupiter, in the
> same manner as before in bringing forward the plate of cakes and
> consecrating the oblation-cake. When all this is done offer the en-
> trails and wine to Ceres. . . .

The following is the Roman ritual for thinning a grove. There is to be the propitiatory sacrifice of a pig with the following formula: "Whether you be a god or a goddess to whom this grove is sacred, as is your due, receive this propitiatory sacrifice of a pig for the violence done to this holy place, and for this purpose, whether I perform the act myself, or someone else performs it on my authority, grant that it may be rightly done. To this end in offering the propitiatory sacrifice of a pig I ask in all faith that you will look with kindly grace on me, my home, my household and my children. To this end accept this propitiatory sacrifice of a pig." If you wish to cultivate the ground offer a second propitiatory sacrifice in the same manner with the additional words "by reason of the work to be done." So long as the work continues see that the ritual is performed each day in a different section of the land. If you omit a day or if some public or private festival is interposed, a further propitiatory offering must be made.

The ceremonial purification of the land must be performed according to the following ritual. Instruct the sacrificial procession of pig, ram and bull to move round the land with the words: "That with the goodwill of the gods all may turn out for the best, I charge you, Manius, to be responsible for the purification of my farm, fields and land by means of this sacrificial procession of pig, ram and bull, directing it to be driven or carried around whatever part you think right." Begin by offering a prayer with a libation of wine to Janus and Jupiter and then speak as follows: "Father Mars, I pray and beseech you to look with kindly favour on me, my home and household; for which purpose I have instructed this sacrificial procession of pig, ram and bull to be driven round my fields, land and farms, that you may avert, keep off and eliminate diseases seen and unseen, barrenness and devastation, and that you may permit my produce, crops, vineyards and plantations to be fruitful and prosper, keep safe my herdsmen and their herds, and grant good health and strength to me, my family and household; for this purpose, for the purification of my farm, land and fields, and for making a purification, accept the sacrifice of this suckling pig, ram and bull. Father Mars for this same purpose accept this suckling pig, ram and bull." Then with the sacrificial knife make a pile of cakes, and see that the oblation-cake be set beside it; then bring forward the victims. The following is the ritual formula for offering the pig, lamb and calf: "For this purpose accept this sacrifice of pig, ram and bull." It is forbidden at this point to mention Mars by name . . . † . . . or the lamb and calf. But if the omens are unfavourable at every point, use the following formula: "Father

Mars, if something has displeased you in the former offering of
suckling pig, ram and bull, I make expiation with this pig, ram and
bull." If there is doubt about one or two, use this formula: "Father
Mars, seeing that you were displeased with the former pig, I make
expiation with this new pig. . . ."

Any kind of dislocation will be cured by the following charm:
take a green reed, four or five feet long, split it down the middle
and get two men to hold it to your hips. Begin the incantation
MOTAS VAETA DARIES DARDARES ASTATARIES DISSUNA-
PITER until the reeds make contact with one another. Pass a knife
over them, and when they meet so that one touches the other,
grasp them in the hand and make cuts to right and left. Then apply
the reeds to the dislocation or fracture and it will be cured. All the
same repeat the incantation daily or, for a dislocation, the following HUAT HAUT HAUT ISTASIS TARSIS ARDANNABOU
DANNAUSTRA.

> Cato *Agriculture* 131-2, 134, 139-141, 160.

There is much here of great interest. Basically we must remember
that Cato was writing a practical textbook. Religion is for him part of
the practicality of farming, and indeed between the instructions
about the offering to Jupiter of the Offering, and the sacrifice of the
pre-harvest pig comes a wholly technical paragraph on layering
fruit-trees. At the same time Cato was a traditionalist and we cannot
doubt that his rituals and formulas go far back into Roman history.
We notice, for example, that Mars does not appear as god of war but,
as in the ritual of Arval Brethren, as a god of agriculture. (How we
may bring together these two sides of his being is much disputed;
perhaps he was a storm-god.) The pre-harvest pig may originally
have been offered to the ancestors, who, living below the earth, both
bless the fertility of the soil and may be disturbed by some false step
in treating the earth. Groves are invariably sacred places—there is a
magnificent description by Lucan of one of Germany—and great religious care must attach to any interference with one. In many ways
the most interesting of these passages has to do with the purification
of the fields. (At the point marked + the Latin does not make sense: I
have assumed a lacuna in our text.) The ceremonial procession of
pig, ram and bull is familiar in sculpture—there is a fine example in
the Forum at Rome. The Ambarvalia is a more formal festival dedicated to the same end. There is an interesting parallel with the medi-
aeval Rogationtide Beating of the Bounds. Naturally too the state festival of the Amburbium (Around the City, instead of Around the
Fields) is similar. Finally at the end of the volume Cato offers a few
country recipes. Dislocations and fractures require more drastic
treatment than other complaints, and a magical incantation is noted.
There is in fact for Cato no boundary between the natural and the
supernatural, and we may, if we like, distinguish between the magi-

cal formula and the religious invocation, but he would not have done so, and though the other passages involve an approach to personally conceived deities, they also involve the precise use of almost mechanical formulas.

The antiquarian M. Terentius Varro (116-27 B.C.) also wrote on agriculture and invoked the appropriate gods.

> They tell us that the gods help those who call on their names. I shall therefore invoke them, not, like Homer and Ennius, calling on the Muses, but on the twelve Gods of the Council, and at that not the gods of the city whose gilded statues stand in the forum, six gods and six goddesses, but the Twelve Gods who give guidance to farmers. First, I call on Jupiter and Tellus who hold in heaven and earth all the fruits of agriculture; they are known as our Almighty Parents, Jupiter is our Father, Tellus is Mother Earth. Secondly, I call on the Sun and Moon whose seasons give the signal for sowing and reaping. Thirdly, I call on Ceres and Liber, because their produce is essential to life; through their agency food and drink emerge from the farm. Fourthly, I call on Robigus and Flora: if they show favour rust will not damage the crops or trees, and there will be no premature flowering: this is why the public festival of the Robigalia has been established in honour of Robigus and the Floralia celebrated for Flora. Similarly, I worship Minerva and Venus, who protect the olive-groves and the garden; the country Vinalia was instituted in the name of Venus. In addition I invoke Lympha and Good Issue, since without water all agriculture is parched and poor, and without success and good issue there is no cultivation, only frustration.
>
> Varro *On Agriculture* 1, 1, 4-6.

> Robigus is the *numen* of rust, a disease of wheat. Flora the eponymous *numen* of flowers, Lympha of water.

Vergil, the former Epicurean, came to appreciate the religion of the countryside as three quotations from *The Georgics* will serve to show.

> What makes the cornfields rejoice, Maecenas, under what star
> it is right to turn the soil and link the vines
> to the elms, how to look after cattle, how to handle
> the flocks, what skill you need for the thrifty bees—

all this is my theme. You most brilliant lights
of the universe, guiding the year as it slips through the sky,
Liber and kindly Ceres, if by your gift the earth
has exchanged Chaonia's acorn for the swelling grain,
and discovered grapes to mix with draughts of water,
and you too, Fauns, visible gods of the farmers
(Come, Fauns, dance, and Nymphs of the Trees with you),
your bounties are my theme. You, too, Neptune, for whom
the earth first produced the neighing steed at the stroke
of your trident; you, Forester, for whom three hundred
snowwhite steers crop Cea's fruitful bushes;
Pan, protector of the sheep, Lord of Tegea, leave
your native woods and the glades of Lycaeus, if you love
your Maenalus, and come in blessing; Minerva, discoverer
of the olive; and you, holy Boy, inventor of the curved plough;
and you, Silvanus, with a young cypress uprooted;
and all you gods and goddesses whose zeal protects our fields,
you who look after young fruit growing unsown,
you who send plentiful rain from the sky for our crops.

                                                        Vergil *Georgics* 1, 1-23.

The Forester is Aristaeus, the Boy Triptolemus.

I must tell of the tough farmers' implements,
Without which the crops could not be sown or grow;
the share and the heavy timber of the curved plough first,
the slow rolling wagons of our Lady of Eleusis,
threshers, harrows, mattocks of impossible weight,
cheap wicker ware from Celeus besides,
hurdles of arbutus and Iacchus' mystic winnowing-fan.
All of these you'll be careful to lay in long beforehand
if you've a proper sense of the worth of the gods' own countryside.

                                                        ibid 1, 160-8.

Divini gloria ruris: Vergil really does mean that the country belongs
to the gods.

Happy the man who could understand the first principles of all
    things,
and trampled beneath his feet all causes of fear,
inexorable fate and the hungry howls of hell.
Blessed by fortune too is he who has come to know the gods of the
    country,
Pan, old Silvanus and the sister Nymphs.

                                                        ibid 2, 490-4.

The first three lines refer to the Epicurean Lucretius, as echoes of that poet's own words make clear. But Vergil changes his word of praise and is perhaps thinking of himself, who has grasped the scientific principles and the gentle friendliness of the philosophy, but has "come to know" the gods of the country beyond that.

Tibullus (c. 48–19 B.C.) gives us a charming picture of the Ambarvalia, the purification of the fields.

Silence, all present. This is a purification of land and crops
　　　　in the traditional rites.
Be with us Bacchus, with delicious grapes hanging from your horns,
　　　　and Ceres crowned with corn.
On this holy day the soil is to rest, the ploughmen to rest,
　　　　the plough to cease work.
Unfasten the yokes. Today the oxen shall stand,
　　　　garlanded, by full mangers.
Everything must be done for the god. No woman must dare
　　　　to spin wool.
Move to a distance, away from the altars, all you
　　　　who last night made love.
The powers above require purity. Come with clean clothes,
　　　　with hands clean from the spring.
Watch how the consecrated lamb moves to the blazing altar,
　　　　followed by the white procession.
Gods of our ancestors, we are cleansing the farmers,
　　　　drive evil from our fences.
Do not let the harvest mock us with tares among the wheat,
　　　　our lambs fear the wolves.
Afterwards the comfortable countryman, confident in his teeming
　　　　fields, will pile logs on the fire,
while a crowd of young slaves, signs of a farmer's prosperity,
　　　　play with the twigs.
My prayers are fulfilled. Look how the marks on the liver
　　　　announce the gods' favour.

　　　　　　　　　　　　　　Tibullus 2, 1, 1-26.

This is a purification with a stress on purity, cleanness, white. It is a holy day and a holiday: even the animals rest. There is an invocation of the right powers, now fully personalized as gods. There is a ritual procession round the bounds of the farm. There is sacrifice on the *do ut des* principle: the sacrificer hopes to receive a gift in return: at the same time the examination of the liver determines whether the god has accepted the gift.

Ovid has left us some attractive pictures of festivals. Here is the Terminalia, in honour of Terminus, the god of the boundary-stone, held on 23 February.

> Once night has passed, give due honour to the god
>> who marks the limits of the fields.
> Terminus, be you a stone or a post in the ground,
>> you have been worshipped for ages past.
> The two owners on opposite sides crown your head,
>> bringing two garlands, two cakes.
> They built an altar. On a broken sherd the farmer's wife brings
>> fire from the warm hearth.
> The old man chops logs, piles them up with neat skill,
>> tries to stick branches in the firm earth,
> then fosters the first flames with dry bark.
>> A boy stands by with a wide basket.
> From this he throws grain three times into the middle of the fire.
>> A little girl offers sliced honeycomb.
> Some hold jars of wine; there's a libation from each on the flames.
>> The congregation watch silently in white.
> Terminus, lord of both lands, is aspersed with the blood of a lamb,
>> and does not refuse a sucking-pig.
> The countryside join in a feast, with simple taste,
>> and hymn you, holy Terminus.
> You mark the bounds of peoples, cities, great empires.
>> Without you every field would mean a lawsuit.
> You are not to be bribed or corrupted with gold;
>> you guard your lands with the integrity of law.
>>> Ovid *Fasti* 2, 639-62.

The sacrifice was no doubt an actual reenactment of the sacrifice offered when the boundary was established: the offerings strengthen the god in his work of defending the agreed boundaries.

3. Ritual and Observance

In thinking of ancient religion we must think primarily not of faith and doctrine, but of ritual and observance, regular festivals, each with its own ceremony, generally, but not invariably, annual, and special observances prescribed for particular purposes.

First, then, a glance at a minute selection from festivals all over the Graeco-Roman world. The geographer and antiquarian Pausanias gives us a number of pictures of festivals from different parts of Greece. Here is a fascinating glimpse of the Athenian ritual called the Bouphonia, the killing of the ox.

> They set barley mixed with wheat on the altar of Zeus Polieus and leave it unprotected. They have an ox in their care ready for sacrifice. This is allowed to go up to the altar and take the grain. One of the priests, entitled the Ox-killer, cuts down the ox, hurls away the axe as the ritual prescribes and runs away. The rest bring the axe to trial as if they did not know the human being responsible.
> Pausanias 1 (Attica), 24, 4.

> It looks as if the ox was a sacred animal and that it was sacrilege to kill it. There is another account of the same ritual, differing slightly in detail, in Porphyry *On Abstinence* 2, 29-30.

Here is Pausanias' account of another Attic festival, the Arrephoria or Symbol-Bearing.

One thing caused me much surprise. It may not be universally known, so I will write an account of it. Two girls live not far from the temple of Athene Polias; the Athenians call them the Arrephoroi. For a period they live close to the goddess; then when the festival is due they perform the following actions by night. They take up on their heads objects which the priestess of Athene gives them to carry—she does not know exactly what she is giving them and they do not know what they are carrying. Not far away, within the walls of the city is a precinct sacred to Aphrodite in the Gardens (so the cult-title), penetrated by a natural underground passage, down which the girls go. They leave the objects they are carrying at the bottom, exchanging them for something else, tightly wrapped up, which they carry back. After this they release the girls and introduce others on to the Acropolis in their place.

Pausanias 1 (Attica) 27, 3.

We know little about this ritual. The girls were aged between 7 and 11, wore white, and spent some time in weaving Athene's sacred robe. The service was a privilege and the girls might have their statues set up on the Acropolis.

The Thesmophoria was a woman's festival held in October in honour of Demeter. It lasted for four days, the first the Ascent of the worshippers to the Temple, the second the Commemoration of Persephone's Descent, the third the Day of Fasting, the fourth the Day of Resurrection on which Mother and Daughter were greeted in their Beauty. Aristophanes' comedy *The Thesmophoriazusae* takes place during the festival, and has echoes of the festival in the songs and dances of the chorus. This little hymn in particular would be appropriate to the final day.

> Come in grace and kindness,
> goddesses, to your grove,
> where no men may look on
> the holy rites, as in torchlight
>   you reveal your immortal faces.
>
> Come, o come, we pray you,
> our Ladies of the Festival.
> If ever you have come in answer
> to our prayers, come now, be present
>   with us here, we implore you.

Aristophanes *Thesmophoriazusae* 1148-59.

At Patrae in Achaea there was a festival called the Laphria.

The people of Patrae celebrate an annual festival in honour of Artemis called the Laphria, for which they use their own local method of sacrifice. Around the altar they place a circle of wood logs, still green, each twenty-four feet long. The driest of the logs are set on the altar in the middle. Just before the date of the festival they build a smooth approach to the altar, covering the altar steps with an earth incline. The opening ceremony is a magnificent procession in honour of Artemis. The virgin priestess rides at the end of the procession in a carriage drawn by deer. The sacrificial ceremony is by tradition deferred to the following day. The festival is an official celebration, and at the same time enthusiastically welcomed by ordinary citizens. They throw alive on to the altar edible birds and sacrificial victims of all kinds, including wild boars, deer and gazelles, wolf-cubs and bear-cubs and even full-grown beasts. On the altar they set the produce of fruit trees as well. Then they set fire to the faggots. At this juncture I have actually watched a bear and some other animals driven by the first blast of the fire to force their way out, and actually strong enough to get away. But those who brought them drag them back again to the pyre. No-one can recollect any of the animals harming anyone.

Pausanias 7 (Achaea), 18, 11-3.

We can see the priestess on a coin in her carriage drawn by stags. Such holocausts as the Laphria were not in fact unique to Patrae.

An inscription from Myconos, datable to about 200 B.C. gives the regulations for the island's festivals.

We invite the gods in the name of Good Fortune. When Cratinus, Polyzelus and Philophron were in office, at the time when the cities had united together, the citizens of Myconos resolved to offer the following sacrifices additional to those previously offered and to rationalize their previous festivals. On the twelve days of Poseidon a ram, handsome, white, uncastrated, shall be offered to Poseidon Temenites. The ram is not to enter the city. The back and shoulders are to be removed; the shoulder is to be offered in sacrifice; the tongue and forelegs are to be given to the priest. On the same day a lamb, white, uncastrated, shall be offered to Poseidon Phykios. The presence of women is forbidden. Out of the income from fishing the Council are to spend twenty drachmas on the purchase of sacrificial offerings. On the same day two fine sows,

one of them pregnant, are to be offered to Demeter Chloe; the back
of the pregnant sow is to be removed. The Council is to pronounce
on the quality of the sows. Those in authority are to assign to the
sacrificing priest the loin and thigh of the second sow, together
with two quarts of pearl-barley and one-and-a-half pints of
wine. . . .

> The inscription goes on to provide similar regulations for other
> months of the year. An island like Myconos naturally honours Posei-
> don, under a variety of cult-titles.

To give a picture of the festivals at Rome it is perhaps best to
take a general conspectus. In 304 B.C. Cn. Flavius placed in the
forum the earliest known *fasti*, that is a calendar showing the days
on which there was or was not a religious interdict on the conduct
of legal business. We have some calendars ranging from the fragmentary to the virtually complete, all dating within less than a
century after the revision of the calendar by Julius Caesar. From
these it has proved possible to reconstruct the table of festivals as it
was in the pre-Caesar period. This means first of all restoring the
regular year to the 355 days assigned to months before Caesar's re-
forms, and accepting the assumption that in the post-Caesar calendars the parts of the months in larger letters were those inherited
from Republican times. What follows then is a reconstruction of
the Republican calendar by W. Warde Fowler (based on Momm-
sen's work) in his well-known book, *The Roman Festivals*, derived
from the collection of thirty inscriptions. It should be added that
we can be fairly certain that the calendar festivals had been unchanged for centuries before Caesar. Except for the names of the
months, and the use of Arabic numerals, I have not translated. De-
tails of interpretation will be found in the notes which follow.

MARCH			**APRIL**		
1 KAL.	NP		1 KAL.	F	
2	F		2	F	
3	C		3	C	
4	C		4	C	
5	C		5 NON.	C	
6	NP		6	NP	

MARCH

7 NON.	F	
8	F	
9	C	
10	C	
11	C	
12	C	
13	EN	
14	NP	EQUIRRIA
15 EID.	NP	
16	F	
17	NP	LIBERALIA AGONIA
18	C	
19	N	QUINQUATRUS
20	C	
21	C	
22	N	
23	NP	TUBILUSTRIUM
24	Q.R.C.F.	
25	C	
26	C	
27	NP	
28	C	
29	C	
30	C	
31	C	

APRIL

7	N	
8	N	
9	N	
10	N	
11	N	
12	N	
13 EID.	NP	
14	N	
15	NP	FORDICIDIA
16	N	
17	N	
18	N	
19	N	CEREALIA
20	N	
21	NP	PARILIA
22	N	
23	NP	VINALIA
24	C	
25	NP	ROBIGALIA
26	F	
27	C	
28	NP	
29	C	

MAY

1 KAL.	F	
2	F	
3	C	
4	C	
5	C	
6	C	
7 NON.	F*	
8	F	
9	N	LEMURIA
10	C	
11	N	LEMURIA
12	NP	
13	N	LEMURIA
14	C	
15 EID.	NP	
16	F	
17	C	
18	C	

JUNE

1 KAL.	N	
2	F	
3	C	
4	C	
5 NON.	N	
6	N	
7	N	
8	N	
9	N	VESTALIA
10	N	
11	N	MATRALIA
12	N	
13 EID.	NP	
14	N*	
15	Q.S.T.D.F.	
16	C	
17	C	
18	C	

	MAY			JUNE	
19	C		19	C	
20	C		20	C	
21	NP	AGONIA	21	C	
22	N		22	C	
23	NP	TUBILUSTRIUM	23	C	
24	Q.R.C.F.		24	C	
25	C		25	C	
26	C		26	C	
27	C		27	C	
28	C		28	C	
29	C		29	F	
30	C				
31	C				

		JULY				AUGUST	
1	KAL.	N		1	KAL.	F	
2		N		2		NP	
3		N		3		C	
4		NP		4		C	
5		NP	POPLIFUGIA	5	NON.	F	
6		N		6		F*	
7	NON.	N		7		C	
8		N		8		C	
9		N		9		F	
10		C		10		C	
11		C		11		C	
12		C		12		C	
13		C		13	EID.	NP	
14		C		14		F	
15	EID.	NP		15		C	
16		F		16		C	
17		C		17		NP	PORTUNALIA
18		C		18		C	
19		NP	LUCARIA	19		FP*	VINALIA
20		C		20		C	
21		NP	LUCARIA	21		NP	CONSUALIA
22		C		22		EN	
23		NP	NEPTUNALIA	23		NP	VOLCANALIA
24		N		24		C	
25		NP	FURRINALIA	25		NP	OPICONSIVIA
26		C		26		C	
27		C		27		NP	VOLTURNALIA
28		C		28		C	
29		C		29		F	
30		C					
31		C					

SEPTEMBER

1 KAL.	F	
2	F	
3	F	
4	C	
5 NON.	F	
6	F	
7	C	
8	C	
9	C	
10	C	
11	C	
12	N*	
13 EID.	NP	
14	F	
15	N*	
16	C	
17	C	
18	C	
19	C	
20	C	
21	C	
22	C	
23	F	
24	C	
25	C	
26	C	
27	C	
28	C	
29	F	

OCTOBER

1 KAL.	N	
2	F	
3	C	
4	C	
5	C	
6	C*	
7 NON.	F	
8	F	
9	C	
10	C	
11	NP	MEDITRINALIA
12	C	
13	NP	FONTINALIA
14	EN	
15 EID.	NP	
16	F	
17	C	
18	C	
19	NP	ARMILUSTRIUM
20	C	
21	C	
22	C	
23	C	
24	C	
25	C	
26	C	
27	C	
28	C	
29	C	
30	C	
31	C	

NOVEMBER

1 KAL.	F	
2	F	
3	C	
4	C	
5 NON.	F	
6	F	
7	C	
8	C	
9	C	
10	C	
11	C	
12	C	

DECEMBER

1 KAL.	N	
2	N	
3	N	
4	C	
5 NON.	F	
6	F	
7	C	
8	C	
9	C	
10	C	
11	NP	AGONIA
12	EN	

NOVEMBER

13 EID.	NP
14	F
15	C
16	C
17	C
18	C
19	C
20	C
21	C
22	C
23	C
24	C
25	C
26	C
27	C
28	C
29	F

DECEMBER

13 EID.	NP	
14	F	
15	NP	CONSUALIA
16	C	
17	NP	SATURNALIA
18	C	
19	NP	OPALIA
20	C	
21	NP	DIVALIA
22	C	
23	NP	LARENTALIA
24	C	
25	C	
26	C	
27	C	
28	C	
29	F	

JANUARY

1 KAL.	F	
2	F	
3	C	
4	C	
5 NON.	F	
6	F	
7	C	
8	C	
9	NP	AGONIA
10	EN	
11	NP	CARMENTALIA
12	C	
13 EID.	NP	
14	EN	
15	NP	CARMENTALIA
16	C	
17	C	
18	C	
19	C	
20	C	
21	C	
22	C	
23	C	
24	C	
25	C	
26	C	

FEBRUARY

1 KAL.	N	
2	N	
3	N	
4	N	
5 NON.	NP	
6	N	
7	N	
8	N	
9	N	
10	N	
11	N	
12	N	
13 EID.	NP	
14	N	
15	NP	LUPERCALIA
16	EN	
17	NP	QUIRINALIA
18	C	
19	C	
20	C	
21	FP*	FERALIA
22	C	
23	NP	TERMINALIA
24	N	REGIFUGIUM
25	C	
26	EN	

JANUARY			FEBRUARY	
27	C		27	NP EQUIRRIA
28	C		28	C
29	F			

Months: The year began in March as the names of the months Quinctilis (fifth = July) to December (tenth) remind us.

Divisions of the month: The first day is called the Kalends (KAL.), the thirteenth or fifteenth the Ides (EID.), and nine days before the Ides, counting inclusively, i.e., the fifth or seventh, the Nones (NON.).

Days: Each day has attached to it a letter of religious significance, F (*fastus*) means that official business might be transacted on that day with divine blessing. C (*comitialis*) means that the day was *fastus*, but also propitious for the holding of political assemblies. N (*nefastus*) means that the day was utterly unpropitious for the conduct of official business. There are four extended periods of such days: April 5-22, when there was concentration on honouring the powers of growth in the farmland; June 5-14, a period preparatory to harvest; July 1-9, for reasons unknown; and February 1-14, a period of purification. NP is a mysterious sign in the post-Caesar calendars. There is no agreed interpretation of it. It is not certain that it appeared on the republican calendars but I have left it in. It appears to mark days of festivals (though not the Lemuria, Vestalia or Matralia or the Regifugium) and the Ides, sacred to Jupiter; but this leaves one or two unaccounted for. EN (*endotercisus* or *intercisus*) is a day "cut into parts": the morning and evening were *nefasti*, but the middle of the day was *fastus*. Q.R.C.F. (*quando rex comitiavit fas*) means that business might begin only when the king had dissolved the assembly. Q.St.D.F. (*quando stercus delatum fas*) applied only to June 15: it was the day of the ceremonial cleansing of Vesta's house, and came at the end of a long period of *dies nefasti*; "once the refuse was cleared away" it became *fastus*. FP was an entry mysterious to the Romans themselves. It has been suggested that it stands for *fastus principio*, meaning that the early part of the day only was propitious for business. One or two entries which I have marked * differ in different versions of the calendar.

Festivals: It will be noticed that all the festivals except the Equirria, and Regifugium, which commemorates a historical event, fall on odd days. Odd days were lucky days: as Vergil says "The god delights in odd numbers."

March: As its name implies, sacred to Mars, god of agriculture and war. EQUIRRIA: unique in falling on an even day; it may have been transferred back from the next day. It was a day of horse-races, but we know that there was also a ritual driving out of a figure named Mamurius (a form of Mars), a well-known fertility ritual. The horse-race may be something to do with warhorses, or with vegetation-spirits or both. LIBERALIA: festival of the god Liber. AGONIA: unknown; perhaps simply, "day of sacrifice." QUINQUATRUS: fifth day after the Ides; purification of shields of war. TUBILUSTRIUM: purification of trumpets.

April: Month of opening, and of growing crops. FORDICIDIA: offering of pregnant cattle. CEREALIA: festival of Ceres; goddess of growth, especially of grain. PARILIA: festival for shepherds' deity Pales; of ambiguous sex. VINALIA: festival of libations of newly opened wine to Jupiter; later associated with Venus. ROBIGALIA: festival of the *numen* Robigus, the spirit of "rust," a disease of wheat.

May: Month of uncertain meaning. LEMURIA: festival of the dead, of which some account is given in a later chapter. AGONIA: uncertain. TUBILUSTRIUM: purification of trumpets, used for political assemblies as well as war.

June: Another month of uncertain meaning; association with Juno is purely speculative. VESTALIA: festival of Vesta, goddess of the hearth, and of the perpetual fire in the state-hearth. MATRALIA: festival of Mater Matuta, an ancient women's goddess.

July: A period of dangerous heat; there is no apparent connecting-thread between the festivals. POPLIFUGIA: the name seems to mean "flight of the people" but the origin and nature of the festival are uncertain. LUCARIA: meaning and origin unknown. NEPTUNALIA: festival of Neptune. FURRINALIA: festival of unknown goddess Furrina.

August: Storing of corn-harvest and celebrations. PORTUNALIA: festival of Portunus, perhaps a god of harbours or of warehouses. VINALIA: perhaps the ceremonial plucking of the first grapes. CONSUALIA: festival of Consus, spirit of the harvest-store. VOLCANALIA: festival of Volcanus, a fire-god, perhaps to protect the stores from fire in the dry season. OPICONSIVIA: the name seems to bring together Ops, the power of plenty, and Consus. VOLTURNALIA: festival of Volturnus, perhaps a river-god associated with the Tiber.

September: Period of rest after the great August festivals. The great celebration of the games known as *Ludi Romani* (the Roman games) came to fill the gap.

October: Vintage and end of campaigning season. MEDITRINALIA: festival of tasting new wine. FONTINALIA: well-dressing. ARMILUSTRIUM: purification of arms for the winter.

November: Month of ploughing and sowing with no time for festivals.

December: Month of relaxation. AGONIA: uncertain. CONSUALIA: winter rites of Consus, perhaps at a time of store-checking. SATURNALIA: famous festival of Saturnus; this day was the real religious festival; Saturnus was probably an agricultural god. It was a period of jollification and of gifts, which passed into the Christian Christmas, and of a reversal of roles between slaves and masters. OPALIA: festival of Ops, god of plenty. DIVALIA: unknown, except that we are told that it was in honour of an equally unknown Angerona; seemingly something to do with the winter solstice. LARENTALIA: associated by Roman etymologists with a deity Acca Larentia, but presumably originally to do with the Lares as ancestral spirits: seemingly a festival of the dead.

January: Still a month of winter leisure, but with a lull after the great December festivals. AGONIA: unknown. CARMENTALIA: festival of the Carmentes, powers of prophecy, perhaps connected with childbirth.

February: Month of purification. LUPERCALIA: purification ceremony and fertility ritual of great interest in which two young priests dressed in the skins of sacrificed goats, their foreheads smeared with blood from the sacrifice, went round striking the women with strips of skin. QUIRINALIA: festival of Quirinus, god of the Roman people in peaceful assembly. FERALIA: festival of the dead. TERMINALIA: festival of Terminus, god of the boundary-stone, already described. REGIFUGIUM: despite some scepticism I take the appearance of this on an even date to mean that it does commemorate the historical expulsion of the kings from Rome. EQUIRRIA: horse-race, curiously reduplicating that in March.

We have a calendar of military festivals, dating from the first half of the third century A.D., from Dura-Europos.

1 January	. . . .
3 January	In view of the public proclamation and fulfilment of vows, for the safety of our Lord Marcus Aurelius Severus Alexander Augustus and for the eternal duration of the empire of the Roman people, an ox to Jupiter Greatest and Best, a cow to Juno, a cow to Minerva, an ox to Jupiter the Victor. . . a bull to Mars the Father, a bull to Mars the Victor, a cow to Victory. . . .

9 January	In view of the honourable discharge of those returning in full enjoyment of privileges and of the calculation of military pay, an ox to Jupiter Greatest and Best, a cow to Juno, a cow to Minerva, a cow to Wellbeing, a bull to Mars the Father. . . .
10 January	For the birthday of the Divine Lady. . . an act of prayer.
. . January	For the birthday of Lucius Seius Caesar Father-in-law of the Augustus, an ox to the Genius of Lucius Seius Caesar Father-in-law of the Augustus.
24 January	For the birthday of the Divine Hadrian, an ox to the Divine Hadrian.
28 January	For the victories of the Divine Severus in Arabia, Adiabene and especially Parthia, and for the Imperial Rule of the Divine Trajan, a cow to Victory over Parthia, and an ox to the Divine Trajan.
4 February	For the Imperial Rule of the Divine Antoninus the Great. . . an ox to the Divine Antoninus the Great.
1 March	For the birthday celebrations of Mars, Father and Victor, a bull to Mars, Father and Victor.
6 March	For the Imperial Rule of the Divine Marcus Antoninus and the Divine Lucius Verus, an ox to the Divine Marcus and an ox to the Divine Lucius.
13 March	In view of the conferring of the title of Commander-in-Chief on the Commander-in-Chief Caesar Marcus Aurelius Severus Alexander, an ox to Jupiter, a cow to Juno, a cow to Minerva. . . an ox to Mars; and in view of the first proclamation as commander-in-chief by the soldiers of the Augustus, the commander-in-chief, Caesar Marcus Aurelius Severus Alexander Augustus, an act of prayer.
14 March	In view of the conferring of the titles Augustus, the Father of his country and High Priest on Alexander our Augustus, an act of prayer; a bull to the Genius of our Lord Alexander Augustus.
19 March	For the first day of the Five-Day Festival, an act of prayer; the same acts of prayer to be repeated for the 23rd.
4 April	For the birthday of the Divine Antoninus the Great, an ox to the Divine Antoninus.

9 April	For the Imperial Rule of the Divine Pius Severus, an ox to the Divine Pius Severus.
11 April	For the Birthday of the Divine Pius Severus, an ox to the Divine Pius Severus.
21 April	For the Birthday of Rome the Eternal City, a cow to Rome the Eternal City.
26 April	For the birthday of the Divine Marcus Antoninus, an ox to the Divine Marcus Antoninus.
7 May	For the Birthday of the Divine Julia Maesa, an act of prayer to the Divine Julia Maesa.
10 May	For the crowning of the standards with roses, an act of prayer.
12 May	For the Games in honour of Mars, a bull to Mars, Father and Avenger.
21 May	In view of the proclamation of the Divine Severus as Commander-in-Chief, an act of prayer.
24 May	For the Birthday of Germanicus Caesar, an act of prayer to the Memory of Germanicus Caesar.
31 May	For the crowning of the standards with roses, an act of prayer.
26 June	In view of the conferring of the title Caesar on our Lord Marcus Aurelius Severus Alexander and his reception of the cloak of manhood, a bull to the Genius of Alexander Augustus.
1 July	In view of the first appointment as consul of Alexander our Augustus, an act of prayer.
4 July	For the Birthday of the Divine Matidia, an act of prayer to the Divine Matidia.
10 July	For the Imperial Rule of the Divine Antoninus Pius, an ox to the Divine Antoninus Pius.
12 July	For the Birthday of the Divine Julius, an ox to the Divine Julius.
23 July	For the day of the Festival of Neptune, an act of prayer and sacrifice.
1 August	For the Birthday of the Divine Claudius and the Divine Pertinax, an ox to the Divine Claudius and an ox to the Divine Pertinax.
5 August	For the Games in Honour of Wellbeing, a cow to Wellbeing.
. . August	For the Birthday of Mamaea Augusta, Mother of our Augustus, a cow to the Juno of Mamaea Augusta.
. . August	For the Birthday of the Divine Marciana, an act of prayer to the Divine Marciana.

31 August	For the Birthday of the Divine Commodus, an ox to the Divine Commodus.
7 September	. . . .
18 September	For the Birthday of the Divine Trajan and for the Imperial Rule of the Divine Nerva, an ox to the Divine Trajan and an ox to the Divine Nerva.
19 September	For the Birthday of the Divine Antoninus Pius, an ox to the Divine Antoninus.
. . September	For the Birthday of the Divine Faustina an act of prayer to the Divine Faustina.
23 September	For the Birthday of the Divine Augustus, an ox to the Divine Augustus.
17 December	. . . an act of prayer; the same acts of prayer to be repeated for the 23rd.

Feriale Duranum

10 Jan: Divine Lady, unknown. 4 Feb: the Great, Caracalla.
19 Mar: Five-Day Festival, the Quinquatrus, to Minerva.
10 May: See A.S. Hoey, "Rosaliae Signorum," *Harvard Theological Review* 30 (1937) 15-35. 21 May: reading uncertain, perhaps Pius rather than Divine. 4 July: Matidia, Trajan's niece and Hadrian's mother-in-law. August: Juno is here the feminine correlative of Genius. August: Marciana, Trajan's sister and Matidia's mother. 17 Dec: The Saturnalia; for a full discussion see R.O. Fink, A.S. Hoey, W.F. Snyder, "The Feriale Duranum," *Yale Classical Studies* 7 (1940) 1-222. The dominance of the military calendar by the Imperial Cult is noteworthy. It will be noted that it stretches right back to Julius, Augustus and Claudius. Political Religion will be the subject of Chapter 4 below. Here it is important to see that military religion did not consist of pious pep-talks but of observances.

For a picture of sacrificial ritual we cannot do better than go to Homer.

They speedily set in order a glorious
sacrifice to the god around the well-built altar,
ritually cleansed their hands and took up the grain-offering.
Then Chryses raised his arms and prayed in a loud voice
"Here me, Lord of the Silver Bow, Defender of Chryse
and sacred Cilla, mighty lord of Tenedos.
If in the past you heard my prayers

and did me honour and struck the Achaean forces grievously,
so now again bring my wish to fulfilment.
Now save the Danaans from this cruel pestilence."
   He spoke in prayer, and Pheobus Apollo heard him
But when they had prayed and thrown the grain on the altar,
they drew back the victims' heads, slit their throats, flayed them,
cut meat from the thighs and covered them in fat,
making a double fold, and laying raw meat on top.
The old man burned these on a spit, and poured a libation
of red wine. The young men stood by, holding forks.
When they had burnt up the thighs and sampled the offal,
they carved up the rest and put it on spits
and roasted it carefully, and unskewered the pieces.
When the work was done and the meal ready,
they set to enthusiastically, all with a fair share.

Homer Iliad 1, 447-68.

Sacrifices to the gods above were performed on or by a raised altar,
and the victim's head was pulled back so that the neck was exposed
to the sky. White victims were used. For sacrifices to the gods below,
the victims were black, and they were dispatched head down above a
trench. The Greeks were at no time great meat-eaters, and the op-
portunity of eating meat would largely come at occasional religious
sacrifices.

Apollonius of Rhodes has a vivid account of an expiation-
ceremony for Jason and Medea, which though it is set in the heroic
age is a basic account of acts of atonement of any period:

Silently, unspeaking, they darted to the altar
and sat in the manner prescribed for wretched suppliants.
Medea hid her face in her two hands,
Jason planted in the earth the great hilted sword,
with which he had killed Aeetes' son. They never raised
their eyes to look Circe in the face. Immediately she recognised
the doom of exile and pollution of murder.
So in reverence for the rule of Zeus, the god of suppliants,
mighty in anger and mighty in salvation when men take life,
she set about the sacrifice by which suppliants for acts
of violence are made clean when they approach the altar.
First in expiation for the unatoned murder
she held over them a piglet born of a sow whose days
still swelled with motherhood, cut its throat,

and sprinkled the blood on their hands. Next she offered
other libations in appeasement, invoking Zeus
the Purifier, protector of blood-guilty suppliants.
Her nymph attendants, her ministers in everything,
carried all the defilements out from the palace together.
She stayed within by the altar, burning round cakes
and atonement-offerings (no wine!) with prayers to avert
the dead Furies' anger, and for Zeus
to be appeased, and look kindly on them both,
suppliants whether for a stranger's death
or for hands polluted with a kinsman's blood.

Apollonius of Rhodes 4, 693-717.

Aspersion with a pig's blood was a regular ritual of purification. On a famous vase we see Orestes receiving a like cleansing, and it was part of the initiation ritual at Eleusis.

Even entry into a temple had its own statutory ritual attached, as may be seen from the inscription relating to the temple of Athene Nikephoros in Pergamum.

These are the rules of purification for entry into the temple of the goddess, whether for citizens or others: they must abstain from their own wife or husband for that particular day, and from the wife or husband of another for two days, and must perform the ceremonial ablutions. Similarly they must abstain for two days from contact with a dead body or a woman in childbirth. After a funeral ceremony they must receive ritual aspersion and entry through the gate where the holy water vessels stand, and they shall be purified the same day.

W. Dittenberger *Sylloge*[3] 982.

From Rome we may take the ritual for the marking out of a *templum*, an area of dedicated ground and the sky above.

On earth the word *templum* is applied to a place delimited by a particular formula for purposes of augury or auspices. The formula is not identical in every instance. On the citadel it runs:

Holy ground and wilderness be mine up to
where I have named them religiously.

Of whatever kind that true tree is, which
    I believe I have stated, let my holy ground
    and wilderness extend to the left.
Of whatever kind that true tree is, which
    I believe I have stated, let my holy ground
    and wilderness extend to the right.
Between these points let there be holy
    ground for direction, for observance, for
    interpretation, as I believe I have
    religiously stated.

             Varro *On the Latin Language* 7, 8.

The reading and meaning of the Latin are quite uncertain, but the general principles are clear. A rectangular area is ceremonially determined, marked out by trees or similar objects, and it is within this ground or corresponding sky that omens are valid. *Templum* literally means something which is cut off or marked out. I have rendered it "holy ground." It is not clear why the holy ground is wilderness. Varro says that some authorities simply took it as "consecrated" but seems to suggest a view of his own that it arises from country districts where the holy ground is not to be used for agriculture.

Livy, here, in telling the story of a treaty between Rome and Alba Longa purporting to belong to the seventeenth century, recounts a very ancient religio-political ritual which evidently lasted to his own day.

Different treaties involve different terms, but the ritual is always the same. Our sources tell us that it was used on this occasion, and there is no record of an earlier treaty. The fetial priest demanded of King Tullus, "Your majesty, do you command me to strike a treaty with the Fulfilling Father of the people of Alba?" "I do," said the king. "Your majesty," he went on, "I require of you the sacred plant." The king replied, "Take a holy herb." The fetial brought a holy herb from the citadel. Then he asked the king, "Your majesty, do you appoint me the royal envoy of the citizens, the people of Rome, together with my brothers and my sacred vessels?" The king made answer: "In so far as it may be done without prejudice to myself and to the citizens, the people of Rome, I do." The fetial's name was M. Valerius; he appointed Sp. Fusius Fulfilling Father by touching his head and hair with the sacred herb. The Fulfilling Father is responsible for seeing that the oath is fulfilled and the treaty finally ratified; he achieves this in a long verse incantation which there is no room to quote. The terms are then read aloud, and he says, "Jupiter, listen, Fulfilling Father of the people of Alba, listen, people of Alba. As these terms have been read aloud in public from beginning to end out of these documents without malice aforethought and as they have been clearly understood on this day in this place, the people of Rome will not be the first to break these conditions. If the people of Rome are the first to break these conditions by vote of the people with malice aforethought, then, almightly Jupiter, do you strike down the people of Rome as I shall on this day in this place strike down this pig; as your power and might are stronger may you strike the more strongly." With these words he struck the pig with a flint. Similarly the people of Alba pronounced their own formulas and ratified their own oath through the agency of their dictator and religious officials.

Livy 1, 24, 3-9.

The *fetiales* were a brotherhood of priests charged with just such offices as these, the religious sanctions of peace and war and public affairs generally. The *pater patratus* or Fulfilling Father was one of the brotherhood who bore special responsibility for the ratification. The flint-knife is interesting: it suggests a very old ritual.

Livy also gives an account of the ritual used in declaring war.

However, as Numa had instituted religious rituals for time of peace, he desired to hand down rituals for war, so that there might be proper rites for the conduct and declaration of war alike. He therefore copied from the ancient people of the Aequicoli the procedure which the fetials now have for demanding redress. When the envoy reaches the territory of the people from whom redress is being demanded, he covers his head with a woollen scarf and says: "Listen, Jupiter; listen, frontiers of—" (naming the people concerned), "listen, justice. I am an envoy of the people of Rome, appointed by the people. I come in religious piety as an ambassador. See that my words have authority." Then he goes through the list of demands. Next he calls on Jupiter as his witness with the words, "If irreligiously and impiously I make demands that these men and these objects be handed to me, then never permit me to enjoy my native land." He goes through these same words as he crosses the frontier, then to the first person he meets, then on entering the city-gate, then after reaching the city-centre, with only minor verbal changes in the formula and form of the oath. If his demands are not met, after the passage of the traditional number

of thirty-three days, he declares war using these words: "Listen,
Jupiter, and you, Janus Quirinus, and all you gods of heaven and
earth and the underworld, listen. I call you to witness that this
people "—naming them—" show no justice and refuse just restitu-
tion. On this matter within our own land we will take counsel of
our elders how to obtain our just rights." Then the envoy returns
to Rome to a consultation. Without delay the king would consult
with the senate, using approximately this formula: "Concerning
the things, suits and causes which the Fulfilling Father of the citizens of the people of Rome has addressed to the Fulfilling Father
of the Ancient people of Latium and the men of the Ancient people
of Latium, things which they have not restored, delivered or performed, things which by right should be restored, delivered or
performed"—turning to the man whose views he traditionally
solicited first—"speak your mind." He would reply: "My mind is
that those things must be called for by war in holiness and righteousness. This I support; to this I give my vote." Next the views of
others were solicited in turn, and once the majority of those present acceded to the same policy, war was agreed. It was the traditional practice for the fetial priest to take a spear with a tip either of
iron or hardened in flame, and coated with blood, to the frontier of
the other nation, and to declare in the presence of three adult
males: "Whereas the tribes of the Ancient Peoples of Latium and
the men of the Ancient People of Latium have been guilty of hos-
tile acts against the citizens, the people of Rome, and whereas the
citizens, the people of Rome, have authorized war against the
Ancient People of Latium; and the senate of the citizens, the
people of Rome, has declared, agreed and voted war against the
Ancient People of Latium, in consequence I and the people of
Rome declare and make war upon the tribes of the Ancient People
of Latium and the men of the Ancient People of Latium." This
said, he would throw the spear into their territory. At that period
this was the form of demanding reparation from the people of
Latium, and declaring war upon them, and the form was handed
on to subsequent generations.

Livy 1, 32, 5-14.

Here again, recorded by the antiquarian Macrobius, is a formula
directed against the gods of a besieged city.

Whether it be a god or a goddess under whose protection the
people and state of Carthage stand, and you, almighty god who
are charged with the protection of this city and this people, I pray

you, I invoke you, I ask your grace that you abandon the people and state of Carthage, leave behind their buildings, temples, holy places and city, and go away from them; that you afflict with fear, terror and forgetfulness that people and state; that when you have gone out from among them you come to Rome to me and to my people; that our buildings, temples, holy places and city may win your favour and acceptation instead; and that you take under your care me and the people of Rome and my soldiers in such a way that we may know and realize it. If you do this I make a vow that I will build you temples and celebrate games in your honour.

Macrobius 3, 9, 7-8.

Carthage is of course a representative enemy. The formula was accompanied by a sacrifice and the taking of auguries.

This would be followed by the formula of devotion.

Father Dis, Vejovis, Powers of the Dead, or whatever be the name under which it is right to invoke you, I call on you all to fill with panic, fear and terror the city of Carthage and her army which I believe myself to be naming to you; and pray that, for these men who are proposing to bring arms and weapons against our legions and our army, you will dismiss their army, these enemies, these men, their cities and temples, and all who live in those places, regions, lands and cities take from them the light of day; and that, for the army of our enemies, and the cities and lands of those whom I believe myself to be naming to you, you treat those cities and lands, and the persons and lives of the people as devoted and consecrated to you by those laws whereby enemies are so devoted. I hand them over and devote them as substitutes for me, for my personal commitment, and for my office of magistrate, for the people of Rome, and for our army and legions, so that you may allow me, my personal commitment, my authority, and our legions and army involved in this enterprise, to prosper and be successful. If you enable me to know, realize and understand that this is so, then whoever has made this vow, wherever he has made it, let it be ratified with three black sheep. Mother Earth, and you, Jupiter, I call to witness.

Macrobius 3, 9, 10-11.

Black victims as always to the gods of the underworld. Dis: the Greek Pluto. Vejovis: Italian underworld god. The formula is authorized for dictators and commanders-in-chief. The mention of Mother Earth was accompanied by touching the ground with both hands, the name of Jupiter with raising the hands to the sky, the vow itself with hand on breast.

A passage in the elder Pliny shows the store which the Romans set by precise ritual formulation.

> Man can provide his own remedies, and the first of them raises a major unsolved question: have words, have formulaic spells any power? If they do, then the fact ought to be generally recognized. Ask intellectuals individually; they hold no such belief; but unconsciously it is universally accepted. It is regarded as useless to offer sacrifice without a prayer: the gods have not been duly consulted. Besides different language is used for securing favourable omens, for averting evil, or invoking support for an enterprise. We notice that our chief magistrates use set prayers. No word must be omitted or out of turn, so each phrase is read from a book for the magistrate to repeat, an official is appointed to keep a strict check, another is authorized to ensure silence, a musician is playing to shut out external noises. There are some remarkable records of both going wrong, of ill-omened noises abnegating the prayer and of mistakes in the prayer itself, resulting within the entrails in the sudden disappearance of reduplication of the head of the liver or the heart while the victim was standing there. There has survived a most important example of a ritual formula which the Decii, father and son, used in devoting themselves. Also extant are the words of the plea of innocence used by the Vestal Tuccia against a charge of unchastity when she carried water in a sieve in the year A.U.C. 609. Our own generation has actually seen a man and woman from Greece, and members of other nations with whom we were at war, buried alive in the Cattle Market. The Master of the College of Fifteen generally goes through the prayer for this ceremony clause by clause. If you read it you are bound to admit the power of formulaic prayer; the outline of eight hundred and thirty years is a complete indication of it. We hold today that our Vestal Virgins can use prayer to root to the ground runaway slaves so long as they have not got clear of the city. If the principle is once accepted that the gods listen to any prayers or are affected by any form of words, then the whole problem is solved.
>
> Pliny the Elder 28, 3, 10-3.

The story of the Decii is told by Livy (8, 9; 10, 28); that of Tuccia by Valerius Maximus (8, 1); the year was 145 B.C.

Another interesting ritual is recorded by Livy from the early

years of the war with Hannibal. This was the Sacred Spring. Livy
quotes the words in which the proposition was laid before the
people.

> Is it your will and decree that this be so done? If the state of the
> people of Rome, the citizens, as I will in this vow, be preserved
> safely for the next five years in these present wars, the war of the
> people of Rome with the people of Carthage, and the wars with
> the Gauls to the south of the Alps, then the citizens, the people of
> Rome, promise as a gift all that the spring produces from the herds
> and flocks of pigs, sheep, goats and cattle, and all that pertains to
> no other god shall be sacrificed to Jupiter on a day to be deter-
> mined by the senate and people. Let him who offers sacrifice sac-
> rifice on what day and with what ritual he choose. Whatever his
> method of offering sacrifice, let it be counted well done. If the in-
> tended sacrificial victim dies, let it be outside the vow, and let
> there be no offence. If anyone unwittingly harm or kill the victim,
> let there be no blame. If anyone steal the victim, let there be no
> guilt on the people as a whole or on the one suffering the theft. If
> sacrifice be unwittingly offered on a day of bad omen, let it be
> counted well done. Whether the sacrifice be offered by night or
> day, by slave or free man, let it be counted well done. If sacrifice be
> offered prematurely without the authority of the senate and
> people, let the people as a whole be free from guilt.
>
> Livy 22, 10, 2-7.

Roman religion was very particular about observances, and we
have full accounts of the highly circumscribed lives lived by the
Vestal Virgins and by the Priest of Jupiter.

> The Pontifex Maximus was responsible for interpreting and pro-
> nouncing on the Divine, or rather for the organization of sacred ri-
> tual, with a general responsibility for public ceremonies and also
> for the supervision of private sacrifices, preventing any departure
> from tradition and giving guidance as to the proper worship or
> prayer. He was charged also with the supervision of the sacred
> virgins called Vestals. Tradition credits Numa with the consecra-
> tion of the Vestal Virgins and in general with the religious ritual
> associated with the undying fire which is in their office; it is not
> clear whether he thought of the nature of fire as pure and incor-
> ruptible and therefore to be in the care of chaste and undefiled
> people or whether he linked its barren and unfruitful quality with

virginity. . . . Some hold the view that nothing beyond the undying fire is in the care of the sacred virgins, others say that they
guard holy objects in private, which no-one else may look upon.

Originally tradition maintains that Numa consecrated Gegania
and Berenia, and subsequently Canuleia and Tarpeia, and that
Servius added two more making up the number still in operation.
The king decreed a thirty-year period of chastity for the sacred virgins; the first decade is spent in mastering their duties, the second
in performing them, the third in teaching them to others. At the
end of this period anyone who wishes is free to marry, resigning
office and adopting a different way of life. But the story goes that
not many welcome this relaxation, and that things have not
turned out well for those who do so, but that penitence and dejection are their bedfellows for the rest of their lives, implanting in the
rest such religious scruples that they persist in their virginity to old
age and death.

Numa assigned them considerable privileges, for example the
right of making testamentary dispositions in the lifetime of their
father, or conducting business without a guardian, like the
mothers of three children. When they appear in public the *fasces*
accompany them. If they meet a criminal on the way to execution,
the sentence is annulled, provided that the Virgin declares on oath
that the encounter was accidental and not contrived. When they
are being carried in a litter, anyone ducking under the litter is ex-
ecuted. The normal penalty for offences by the Virgins is corporal
punishment administered by the Pontifex Maximus on the bare
flesh of the offender in a dark room with a curtain stretched between them. But a Vestal who has broken her vow of virginity is
buried alive close to the so called Colline Gate. Just within it, inside the city, there is a long mound of earth, known in Latin as the
agger. Under the ground is built a small room, with steps leading
down into it from above. Inside is set a bed with bedclothes, a
lighted lamp, and small helpings of the necessities of life, such as
bread, a jug of water, milk and olive oil, as if they hoped to free
themselves from the curse of destroying by starvation a person
dedicated to the highest religious office. The condemned Vestal is
placed on a litter, covered over completely and fastened with
ropes till no cry is audible outside, and carried through the forum.
The whole population line the route in silence and escort the litter
without speaking in their fear and dejection. It is the most horrify-
ing spectacle, the most accursed day in the life of the city. When
the litter reaches its destination, the attendants untie the ropes,
the spokesman for the priests offers prayer in incomprehensible

words and stretches out his hands to heaven before the final act is irrevocable. He then takes the Vestal, who is completely veiled and places her on the steps which lead down to the room. Then he and the other priests avert their faces. She makes her descent, the steps are removed and the room is covered in with a heap of earth from above till the place is level with the rest of the mound. That is the punishment of those who betray their holy virginity.

Plutarch *Life of Numa* 9-10.

Many religious duties are laid upon the Priest of Jupiter, with many sorts of tabu as well, of which we can read in the volumes *On the Public Priests* and as a subject in Book I of Fabius Pictor. Here is a reasonable summary of those I remember. There is a tabu against the Priest of Jupiter riding on horseback; another against his seeing the "citizens in array" outside the sacred city-boundary (in other words the forces under arms)—which is why the Priest of Jupiter is not usually appointed consul, since wars were the consuls' business. It is never right for the Priest of Jupiter to take an oath. Again, he is not permitted to wear a ring unless the circle is incomplete and there is no bezel. There is a tabu against taking fire from the *flaminia* (the residence of the Priest of Jupiter) except for religious purposes. If a man with hands or feet bound ever enters his house he must be released and his bonds pulled up through the skylight to the roof and let down from there into the street outside. He is not allowed a knot in his cap or belt or any part of his clothes. If a man sentenced to flogging falls at his feet in supplication, there is a religious injunction against the sentence being carried out on that particular day. Only a free man may cut the Priest of Jupiter's hair. It is not usual for the Priest of Jupiter to touch or even mention a she-goat, raw flesh, ivy or beans. He must not pass under a canopy of vines. The feet of the bed he sleeps in must be smeared all over with a thin layer of clay; he must not sleep away from that bed for three nights running; it is strictly forbidden for anyone else to sleep in that bed; at the foot of his bed must stand a box with oblation cakes of different kinds. His nail-parings and hair-clippings are buried in the earth at the root of a fruitful tree. For him every day is sacred. He is not allowed to be in the open air with head bare; Masurius Sabinus has claimed that indoors this has only recently been authorized by the political college; it is suggested that there have been other relaxations and excusals from religious observances. He is not permitted to touch bread containing yeast. He never takes off his underclothes except in a private room for fear of being naked to the sky, that is the eyes of Jupiter. At a dinner-party no-one takes precedence over the

Priest of Jupiter except the King of Sacrifice. If he loses his wife, he has to resign. The priest's marriage cannot be annulled except by death. He never goes into a burial-ground, and never touches a dead body, but there is no tabu against his attending funerals.

Aulus Gellius 10, 15, 1-25.

> The tabus are of great interest. Jupiter is a sky-god, and too close a contact between the sky and its great representative on earth might generate uncontrollable power. The priest must be protected against magic, which might be applied to his hair-clippings or nail-parings or the impress of his body on a bed. Closed rings, knots in his clothes, the binding power of an oath, might confine the divine power till it could only find an explosive release. Contact with slaves or the dead, with a newfangled invention like iron, with the people at war (Jupiter was not a wargod) would be dangerous. And so on.

Two contrasting passages may usefully conclude this section. In the first, a character in Petronius bemoans the result of neglecting religious observances.

> "What'll come of it if there's no concern for this township of ours from omen or gods? I believe it all comes from the gods, damn my family if I don't. No-one believes in heaven, no-one observes a fast, no-one cares a halfpenny for Jupiter. They all shut their eyes and look after number one. In the old days the women would go barefooted in their best clothes, with hair loose and mind pure, up the hill to pray Jupiter for rain. Hey presto, it poured down in buckets—now or never: they all looked like drowned rats by the time they reached home. That's why the gods have gone lame— we've forgotten our religion. So our fields lie. . . ."

Petronius Satyricon 44.

In the second, Clearchus of Methydrium explains his reputation for sanctity.

> I discharge my religious duties and am particular to offer sacrifice at the statutory times. Every month at the new moon I offer flowers and other decorations to Hermes and Hecate and the other images which my ancestors handed down to me, and I honour them with incense, barley and cakes. Every year I perform the public sacrifice. I never neglect a single festival. On these occasions I honour the gods without sacrificing oxen or slaughtering victims, but by whatever offerings are to hand. I am most particular to allot to the

gods the first-fruits of all the seasonal crops which the earth produces. I set some before them, and consecrate some apart. I pay attention to my own wellbeing, and personally put in hand the sacrifice of cattle.

Theopompus FGH 115 F 344=
Porphyry *On Abstinence* 2, 16.

4. Political Religion

Religion embraced politics as it embraced all of life. In any event the state was only the family writ large, as we can see at Rome where Vesta, the spirit of the hearth in every simple cottage, was the goddess who presided over the central hearth of the Roman people, and the Ambarvalia or purification of the boundaries of the farm, was precisely paralleled by the Amburbium or purification of the boundaries of the city.

The forces holding together the Greek city-states were religious: they depended on a common language and a common religion. There was above all the power of Olympian Zeus. His quadrennial festival, the Olympic Games, was a period of truce. The Delphic Oracle of Apollo was another unifying force. There were personal and private consultations, but the Delphic priesthood expected to be consulted on political matters by all the Greek states, and played, for example, an important role in colonization. Herodotus' account of the founding of Cyrene will serve as an example (4, 147-59). One Theras left Sparta and settled on Thera. One of his descendants, Grinnus, was ruler of the island, and went to Delphi with a precautionary sacrifice, to be told to found a city in Africa. He said he was too old, and suggested a companion named Battus. Nothing was done, and Thera suffered severe drought until they obeyed the oracle. In another version Battus ("Stammerer") went to Delphi on a personal consultation about his speech-problems, to be told:

Battus, you've come for a voice, but the Lord Phoebus Apollo
   sends you
to Africa, nurse of flocks, as a founder.

Again nothing happened; again the god showed his anger.
Battus set out, settled on an island off the coast, was unsuccessful,
and went again to Delphi. This time the response ran:

If you know Africa, nurse of flocks, better than I do—
I've been, you haven't—I congratulate you on your wisdom.

Some time later the Cyreneans were encouraging colonists.
The Oracle supported them:

Any who comes to lovely Africa too late
for the allocation of land, will surely be sorry after.

We do not know what the Oracle's interest in Cyrene was, but
the political influence was firm, wide-ranging and considerable.

Each of the Greek city-states had its tutelary god or goddess,
and a treaty between Athens and Samos might be visually depicted
by Hera of Samos and Athene of Athens clasping hands.

A few lines from Aristophanes show as clearly as anything just
what Pallas Athene meant to Athens.

> Pallas, our city's protector,
> ruler of a land of piety,
> a land outstanding among
> all lands in war,
> and poetry, and power,
> come here, attended by
> our true companion
> in war and battle,
> Victory, our friend in the theatre,
> our ally against our enemies.
> Be seen here now.
> We need all your skill
> to bring your servants
> victory, if ever, now.
>
> Aristophanes *The Knights* 581-94.

> The chorus are of course playing on patriotic emotion and hoping to
> transfer it to their own dramatic performance.

That is from the fifth century B.C. Similar emotions were still prevalent in the second century A.D. Aelius Aristides was a professional orator whose main interest for us lies in his hypochondria and his profoundly moving personal relationship to the healing god Asclepius. In A.D. 155 (probably) he delivered a long, popular but somewhat turgid speech at the Panathenaic festival. In the course of it he shows how religion and politics are ineluctably intertwined.

> It is probably best to begin with an exposition of the divine dimension, and go on to the general virtues of these heroes, and finally to their achievements at all periods, whether individual or in alliance with others. I shall recapitulate a little. The gods granted your land the privileges I have already mentioned, and many others as well; it might have been enough to mention the highest of these. This is the only city under the sun which can claim that the highest of the gods contended over it, trying to assert a kind of monarchical right to its acropolis. And they issued a second privilege of equal importance: they entrusted the decision to a jury and judges of the actual occupants of the land, holding it on both sides rather delightful to have judgement given by one's own favourites. Each side presented its token, the sea-surf and the olive-branch. Athene won her case and displayed the branch as a token of victory. Poseidon lost, but did not slacken his enthusiasm. The events that followed were equal signs of the zealous support of both parties. Athene gave the city the gift of supreme wisdom, Poseidon the gift of naval victory over the city's enemies, including those with considerable experience of sea-warfare and a long record of battles and victories. The story is swiftly told. The Goddess, because she secured her majority, gave her name to the city and made it her own, and organized it as her own possession to cope with peace and war alike. She began by the grant of oratory, legislation and a constitution which did not depend on monarchical power. From this came the invention of sciences of all sorts and the introduction of different ways of life. Further she educated them in the use of arms, and clothed them first in the armour in which we now clothe her. She produced chariots for racing and war. The Goddess's associate, in this country, was the first human being to produce,

with her help, a fully-equipped chariot and to display to all horse-manship in its perfection. Next visitations from various gods produced ritual dancing, religious initiation and religious festivals. So honours were paid to the gods, gifts were alike given and received in appropriate form. Apart from contending over the city, the gods gave decisions over the subject of their contention within the city, directing the eyes of all mankind to the city, and aiming to establish there model first principles in every field—just like those who give elementary instruction to children. If the best teachers give the elementary education, there is an excellent prospect for those who copy their example; so the gods hoped that those who followed their own ideal example might turn into complete men, receiving from the gods not just the seeds of wheat and barley, but the seeds of justice and a general way of political and social life. Poseidon sued Ares over his son and won his case before all the gods. The place concerned took its name from this as a record of the event and further persuasive evidence of justice for the rest of mankind. For if you are looking for absolute justice nothing can be found higher than the Areopagus. Just as prophetic waters and exhalations have a potent effect on those subject to divine inspiration, so this place seems to exhale the clear knowledge of justice, as close as humanly possible to divine justice. Everyone respects the Areopagus. Those who lose their case are as contented as those who win, all those in office, all assemblies, above all the commons—all appear as private individuals, bowing to the decisions made in this court. Change, universal in human affairs, has virtually not touched this place alone. It is left as it was, a place where gods and others subsequently may meet in dispute. All men take it as a pattern of justice and give it the deference due to the gods. There was a second trial later: the contenders were mixed, the judges divine. An unfortunate human being, one of the house of Pelops, was confronted with the Holy Goddesses who now dwell by the place. He had taken refuge, appealed to the city, as likely to find there if anywhere humanity and justice. He won the support of the Goddess and was released from his madness.

Aelius Aristides 1, 40-8.

The Goddess's associate is the legendary Erichthonius. The court, from the contest between Poseidon and Ares, received the name Areopagus. The second case is the trial of Orestes, memorably recorded in Aeschylus' drama; the Holy Goddesses are the Avenging Furies. The whole passage is very illuminating in the importance of myth.

To take an example from a smaller town; in 308 B.C. the Macedonians left the town of Eretria. A fragmentary inscription celebrates the occasion in religious terms.

> The priest of Dionysus, Theodotus, Theodorus' son, and the military commanders, Sosistratus, Protomenes' son, Aeschylus, Antandrides' son, and Ithaigenes, Aeschylus' son, have moved as follows. Since on the day of Dionysus' festival the garrison has withdrawn and the people have been liberated, and the democracy and ancestral laws have been restored; as a memorial of this day the Council and People have resolved that all the citizens and inhabitants of Eretria shall wear a garland of ivy at the festival of Dionysus, and that the citizens shall receive their garlands at the public expense, and the Chancellor shall contract for the garlands. The dances shall begin in the honour of Dionysus, and wine. . . .
> W. Dittenberger *Sylloge Inscriptionum Graecarum*[3] 323.

An excellent example of the interaction of religion and politics may be seen in the frieze from the temple of Hecate at Lagina in Caria, now in the Archaeological Museum at Istanbul. The frieze has four separate subjects for its four sides. On the east are episodes from the lives of Zeus and Hecate, including the birth of Zeus clearly envisaged as taking place in Caria. On the south is an Assembly of the local gods of Caria. On the west is the traditional scene of the battle of gods and giants, at one and the same time the triumph of religion over irreligion, and the triumph of Greek civilization over the "barbarians" of the interior. And the north depicts Rome personified establishing an alliance with Stratonicaea and her dependents. The whole may be dated to about 100 B.C.

In the Hellenistic Age, when men began to suffer from what J.B. Bury, followed by G. Murray, called a "failure of nerve," the old religions began to crumble, and men looked for new focal points for their adoration. The old gods had been humans, removed from the scourge of death, and with their powers raised to the nth degree: man had made God in his own image, had projected himself on the universe as it were. But the new world-rulers wielded powers immeasurably greater than the old city-state could have dreamed of, powers raised, as it were to the $(n + 1)$th degree. It was natural that they should appear as present divinities; their power to bless or destroy was real and visible. There were precedents in those the Greeks called heroes, demigods, themselves the sons of gods, who might, like Heracles or Asclepius, be raised to full godhead in reward for their services to mankind. Others too, such as city founders, might be raised to heroic honours, and the Hellenistic monarchs from Alexander onwards were undeniably city-founders, witness the Alexandrias, Cassandreias, Ptolemaises, Berenices, Antiochs, Eumeneias and similarly derived names scattered over the eastern Mediterranean and far into Asia. One of the (to us) oddest cases is recorded by Pausanias.

> At the previous Olympian festival it is recorded that Cleomedes of Astypalaea killed Iccus of Epidaurus in a boxing-match. He was disqualified by the referees for foul play. The loss of his victory drove him out of his wits. He returned to Astypalaea, burst into the school containing about sixty children, and pulled down the pillar supporting the roof, which fell upon the children. The citizens pursued Cleomedes with stones, and he took refuge in the temple of Athene, jumping into a chest which was standing in the sanctuary and pulling the lid down over his head. The Astypalaeans struggled and struggled in their unsuccessful attempts to open the chest. In the end they smashed the panels of the chest—but failed to find Cleomedes, alive or dead. They sent representatives to Delphi to ask what had happened to Cleomedes. The oracle's reply is recorded,
>
> > Cleomedes of Astypalaea is last of the demigods.
> > Honour him with sacrifices: he is no longer a mortal.
>
> so from that moment the Astypalaeans have done reverence to Cleomedes as to a demigod.
>
> Pausanias 6 (Elis), 9, 6-8.

There were then precedents for demigods, not just as faded gods but as exalted humans.

In 307 B.C. Demetrius Poliorcetes (the Besieger) visited Athens. They actually gave him the Parthenon as his palace, and sang a processional hymn in his honour.

The greatest, the dearest of the gods,
are here in our city.
The fullness of him has brought here together
Demeter and Demetrius.
She comes to celebrate the sacred
Mysteries of the Maiden.
He is here in gladness, handsome, smiling,
as a god should be.
He appears as a revelation, his associates all around,
himself in the centre—
it is as if his associates were the stars,
himself the sun.
Son of Poseidon, mightiest of gods,
and Aphrodite, welcome.
Other gods are far away
or cannot hear,
or do not exist at all, or care nothing for us.
You are present; we can see you,
not carved in wood or stone, but real.
To you we pray.
First bring us peace—we love you dearly—
You have the power. . .

Anon quoted by Athenaeus 6, 253 D.

In Egypt the cult of Sarapis was at first devised as a unifying spiritual force for the Ptolemaic regime, but it was almost too successful, and spread far outside Egyptian territories and Egyptian political influence. Ruler-worship became the binding factor.

In the reign of the young king, who inherited the kingdom from his father, the glorious Lord of the Diadems, who made Egypt strong, who was pious in matters of religion, victorious over his adversaries, who restored the life of mankind, Lord of the Thirty-Year Festivals, Great like Hephaestus, King like the Sun, Great King of Upper and Lower Egypt, child of the Parent-loving Gods, acknowledged by Hephaestus, granted victory by the Sun, living image of Zeus, son of the Sun, Ptolemy the ever-living, beloved by Phtha, in the ninth year, when Aëtus, Aëtus' son, was Priest of Alexander and of the Saviour Gods and of the Brother Gods and of the Benefactor Gods and of the Parent-loving Gods and of the God Manifest and Gracious, and when Pyrrha, Philinus' daughter, was Priestess of Victory for Berenice the Benefactress, and Areia,

Diogenes' daughter, was Processional Priestess for Arsinoë the
Brother-lover, and Irene, Ptolemy's daughter, was Priestess for
Arsinoë the Parent-lover, on the fourth day of the month Xandi-
cus or in the Egyptian calendar the eighteenth day of Mecheir, the
following decree was passed:

The high priests and prophets, and those who enter the sanctuary to robe the gods, and those who wear the hawk's wing, and the
sacred scribes, and all the other priests who gathered at Memphis
in the king's presence from all the shrines of the country for the
anniversary festival of his succession to the throne of Ptolemy the
ever-living, beloved by Phtha, the God Manifest and Gracious,
the throne which he inherited from his father, all these congregated
in the temple at Memphis on this day declared:

Since King Ptolemy the Ever-living, beloved by Phtha, God
Manifest and Gracious, born of King Ptolemy and Queen Arsinoë,
the Parent-loving Gods, has performed many benefactions to the
Temples and those in them and all those subject to his dominion,
being himself from the beginning God, born of a God and Goddess, like Horus, the son of Isis and Osiris, who came to the rescue
of his father Osiris, and in his benevolent disposition towards the
gods has consecrated to the temples revenues of silver and grain,
and has undertaken many expenses so as to lead Egypt into the
light of day and establish the Temples firmly and has shown love
of mankind with all his resources . . . and since he gave many gifts
to Apis and Mnevis and to the other sacred animals in Egypt, con-
sidering what was appropriate for the sacred animals in every respect far more than did his predecessors, offering appropriately
lavish gifts for their funeral ceremonies and for the regular collec-
tions for their special shrines together with sacrifices, festivals and
the other customary observances, and throughout the land preserved the due honours of the temples and of Egypt in accordance
with the laws, and since he equipped the Temple of Apis with rich
offerings presenting a large quantity of gold, silver and precious
stones for the purpose, and since he founded temples, shrines and
altars and restored those requiring attention, having the attitude
of a divine Benefactor in religious matters, and since he made dili-
gent enquiries about the most honoured of the holy places, and
duly restored them during his reign—for all this the gods have
granted him health, victory, power and all other blessings, with
his royal authority continuing to him and his children forever.

With Good Fortune. The priests of all the holy places of the land
have resolved to increase greatly all the existing honours paid to

King Ptolemy the Ever-living, Beloved by Phtha, God Manifest and Gracious, and likewise to his parents the Parent-loving Gods, and to his ancestors the Benefactor Gods and the Brother Gods and the Saviour Gods, and to set up a statue of King Ptolemy the Everlasting, God Manifest and Gracious in the most visible place of every temple, to be called the statue of Ptolemy the Defender of Egypt, and alongside it shall stand the principal god of the temple, handing him an emblem of victory. All this is to be portrayed in the Egyptian manner. The priests shall worship at the images three times a day and provide them with holy robes, and perform all the other ritual traditional to the other gods in the national festivals. And there shall be set up to King Ptolemy, God Manifest and Gracious, born of King Ptolemy and Queen Arsinoë, Parent-loving Gods, a golden statue and shrine in each of the temples, and it shall be placed in the sanctuary with the other shrines, and in the great festivals in which the shrines are brought out and carried in procession, the shrine of the God Manifest and Gracious shall accompany them in procession. . . .

W. Dittenberger *Orientis Graeci Inscriptiones Selectae* 90.

This is the famous Rosetta stone, which made possible the decipherment of Egyptian hieroglyphics. I have translated the Greek: there are slight variants. There is much more to the same tune. As Paul Wendland said in his famous *Hellenistisch-römische Kultur*, this is a cardinal document for ruler-worship. The date of the inscription is 196 B.C. The divine family consists of the Ptolemies and their queens. Ptolemy I was called Saviour, Ptolemy II Brother-lover (Philadelphus), Ptolemy III Benefactor, Ptolemy IV Parent-lover, and the reigning Ptolemy V God Manifest (Epiphanes). There is a fusion of Greek and Egyptian religious myth: for example the Egyptian Phtha was identified with the Greek Hephaestus. What is so interesting about the passage is that there does seem to be a clear distinction between the divine ruler and the other gods.

Equally interesting, but too long to quote in its entirety, is an inscription set up high in the mountains of the Graeco-Persian small independent kingdom of Commagene among figures of the gods by their king Antiochus I, who was reigning in the middle of the first century B.C. A short quotation may give an impression.

For this reason, as you can see, I have here set up these holy images of Zeus-Oromasdes, of Apollo-Mithras-Helios-Hermes, of Artagnes-Heracles-Ares, and of my mother-land Commagene.

From the same stone I have set up my own physical likeness, enthroned among the gracious gods, and have given new life to the
traditional honours of the ancient gods by introducing a new Fortune among them. This is to follow with propriety the example of
divine Forethought, who has often been my visible supporter and
offered beneficent help in the struggles of my reign. I have assigned adequate land and inalienable revenues from it for considerable sacrifices; I have selected priests, so that the divine service
will never lapse, and robed them in vestments appropriate to Persians; I have dedicated the whole of the ceremonial and the canon-
icals in a manner worthy of my Fortune and the majesty of the
Gods. I have enthroned suitable laws to control the administration
of the ceremonial time without end so that all the people of my
kingdom may combine with the ancient and traditional sacrifices
new festivals to the glory of the Gods and to My own honour. . . .
        W. Dittenberger *Orientis Graeci Inscriptiones Selectae* 383.

> The language is pompous and rhetorical. The mixture of Greece and
> Persia is particularly interesting. Oromasdes is Ahura-Mazda, the
> high god of Zoroastrian religion. Mithras is a god of the firmament, a
> mediator, who burst into the Roman world as a saviour-figure; he is
> not really the god of the Sun, though there is some blurring. Artagnes
> is a Persian hero-figure, identified elsewhere with Heracles. The
> king's identification of himself as a god to be worshipped and yet a
> pious worshipper of the other gods is of great psychological interest.

The Roman emperors had plenty of precedents. Julius tempor-
ized: he was toying in lifetime with the divinization which he received after death.

> Julius died at the age of 55 and was added to the number of the
> gods alike by formal proclamation and popular belief. At the orig-
> inal games which Augustus, his successor, presented in honour of
> his deification, a comet shone for seven consecutive nights, ap-
> pearing about an hour before sunset, and was believed to be the
> soul of Caesar after his arrival in heaven. This is why a star has
> been placed upon his forehead in his statue.
>   Suetonius *Julius* 88.

But it was Augustus with his extraordinary political flair who
set the pattern for emperor-worship at Rome. His deification of

Julius allowed him to call himself "son of the divine Julius," and brought him, so to speak, half-way to deification. But, except in Egypt he would not allow himself to be worshipped as an independent god in his lifetime; his name must be coupled with Roma or the Lares or Poseidon; a libation might be poured to his Genius, honour paid to his Peace or his Concord or his Wellbeing. But the mood of reverence was clear.

> . . . whether the birthday of the divine Caesar has brought more joy or blessing, a day which we would rightly account equal to the beginning of the world, if not by nature, at least in practical usefulness, since at a time when everything was falling apart and turning out disastrously, he restored it, and gave the whole world a new look, the world which might have welcomed dissolution if Caesar had not been born as a common blessing to all. The fact of his birth was an end and bound to misery, and we may rightly account it the beginning of real life. Since no-one could enter on any enterprise whether for public or private gain under better auspices than on the day which has proved a blessing to all mankind, and since entry upon public office happens to come at about the same time in all the cities of the province of Asia (evidently a predetermined ordinance of the divine will to be a source of honour to Augustus), and since it is not easy to give thanks commensurate with his beneficent actions without designing some new expression of gratitude suited to all his good deeds, and since men will be the more willing to celebrate the birthday as a general festival if it is associated with the particular pleasure of the inauguration of new officials, it is my proposal that the citizens of all the cities adopt a single universal beginning to the new year in Caesar's birthday, and that this shall be the day for entering office, that is 23 September, so that that day may receive external marks of respect and greater acknowledgement, and may be universally familiar, a day which I regard as likely to confer exceptional blessing on the exercise of office. This decree will have to be formally recorded by the Commonwealth of Asia together with a catalogue of his virtues, so that our intention with regard to doing honour to Augustus may remain in perpetuity. I shall give orders for the decree to be inscribed on a pillar and set up in the temple, having given previous instructions about the detailed enunciations.

Decree of the Greeks in Asia, on a proposal from the High Priest Apollonius, Menophilus' son, from Azanoi. Since the Providence which has controlled the whole of our life, bringing with it an ac-

tive concern and sense of honour, has added the coping-stone to
our life in presenting us with Augustus, whom Providence filled
with virtue so that he might bring benefactions to men, sending
him to us and our successors as a Saviour to put an end to war and
set all in order, and since Caesar, having become manifest, has fulfilled the hopes of earlier generations . . . not only outstripping all
benefactors who preceded him but leaving no hope of outstripping
him in time to come, and since the god's birthday has been the beginning of good news brought through his agency for the whole
world . . . therefore the Greeks in the province of Asia decreed
with Fortune's blessing for their own well-being that the new year
should begin for all the cities on 23 September, the same being
Caesar's birthday. . . .

W. Dittenberger *Orientis Graeci Inscriptiones Selectae* 458.

Particularly interesting in this is the language of the Hellenistic mon-
archies ("Benefactor," "Saviour") and the emergent language of godhead ("Manifest") to the full declaration of Augustus as a god. The
decree which comes from Priene, dates from 9 B.C.: the proconsul
Paulus Fabius Maximus being the proposer. Versions of it (some in
Latin) have been found in Apamea, Eumena and Dorylaeum.

So the pattern was established that an emperor, being a de-
scendant (by blood or adoption) of earlier divine emperors, if he
ruled well, might after death be, as it were, co-opted to the heavenly
senate because of his labours for mankind and "the magnitude of
his benefactions to the whole world." We have a description of the
ritual.

It is the practice of the Romans to deify those of their emperors
who die, leaving children to succeed them. They call the rite apotheosis. Mourning is observed all through Rome, curiously mixed
with festival celebrations and religious worship. They inter the
body of the dead emperor in the ordinary way with a costly funeral.
Then they make a wax image exactly like the dead man, and expose it to view on a large ivory couch spread with cloth of gold and
elevated on a platform, in the entrance-hall of the palace. The
image is pallid like a sick man as it lies there. For most of the day
the whole of the senate sit round the bed on the lefthand side,
clothed in black, and on the right all the women whose husband's
or father's position entitle them to a place of honour. These last
wear no gold jewellery or necklaces but put on plain white clothes

like mourners. These observances extend over seven days. Every day doctors arrive, go up to the bed, and actually examine the patient and announce that he is growing steadily worse. When they decide that he is dead, the noblest member of the equestrian order and carefully selected young men of senatorial rank take up the bier, carry it along the sacred way, and expose it to public view in the old forum, at the place where the magistrates of Rome take the oath at the end of their term of office. On either side stands are constructed with tiers. Two choirs stand on these, one formed of children from upper-class families, and opposite one of women of repute. Each sings hymns and praise-songs for the dead man, modulated in tones of mournful solemnity.

Next they carry the bier out of the city to the Campus Martius. Here in the widest section of the open space there has been erected a square structure, built entirely of huge logs, rather like a house. This is completely filled with brushwood, and ornamented outside with gold-embroidered hangings, ivory statues and a variety of pictures. On top of this erection a similar but smaller one is built, with open doors and windows, and above it a third and fourth in diminishing sequence, with the smallest of all on top. In form the structure is like those lighthouses which dominate harbours, and guide ships in the dark to safe berths, and which go by the general name of Pharos. They take the bier up to the second storey and set it down there, heaping up every sort of aromatic spice and incense and every kind of fragrant fruit, herb or juice. Every nation, every city, every person of prominence vie with one another in offering these last gifts in honour of the emperor. When a vast heap of these aromatics is collected and the entire chamber filled with them, there is a cavalry procession around the pyre and the whole equestrian order circle round in formation using the pace and rhythm of the Pyrrhic dance. Chariots move round in the same formation, their drivers wearing the purple-fringed toga, and carry figures wearing masks resembling the most distinguished Roman emperors and military commanders. When this part of the ritual is complete the heir to the throne applies a torch to the construction, and the others fire the pile from all sides. The whole thing goes up in flames without difficulty in view of the quantity of brushwood and aromatics piled up inside. Then from the smallest storey at the very top, as from a pinnacle, an eagle is released to mount into the sky together with the fire, taking the emperor's soul from earth to heaven, as the Romans believe. Thereafter he is worshipped with the other gods.

Herodian 4, 2.

This account is linked to the apotheosis (the Greek word was adopted in Latin) of Septimius Severus in A.D. 211. It differs in some particulars from the similar account of the deification of Pertinax in Dio Cassius 74, 4; there may have been variants on different occasions. We also see the pyre, and indeed the eagle on coins (e.g., *BMC* 4, 764; 5, 423, 428). The ceremony is discussed in an important article: E. Bickermann, "Die römische Kaiserapotheose", *Archiv für Religionswissenschaft* 27 (1929) 1-34.

But the Romans had long been adept at the use of religion to subserve political ends. The Greek historian Polybius (second century B.C.) saw it.

I fancy that the power of the Romans is sustained by the very factor which the rest of mankind criticize so strongly. I am referring to their religiosity. It has been dramatized, and introduced into public and private life to a most powerful extent. Many find this inexplicable. My view is that it was done because of the man in the street. A state composed of philosophers might be able to do without this expedient. But the commons everywhere are unstable, full of lawless passion, irrational temper and violent disposition. Nothing is left but to hold them under control by fears of the unseen and dramatic touches of that sort. There was nothing irrational about our fathers when they imposed on the commons beliefs about the gods and after-life. We are much more irrational in eliminating them.

Polybius 6, 56.

Five centuries and more later the Christian Augustine headed a chapter of *The City of God* (4, 32) with the words "On what view of expediency the rulers of the nations wanted false religions to be permanent among the peoples subject to them."

After the sack of Rome by the Gauls in 390 B.C. there was some talk of emigrating to Veii. Livy puts into the mouth of Camillus a powerful dissuasive based on the religious destiny of Rome. The ideas in it must be seen as part of Augustus' reassertion of religious values, but also as part of a very ancient tradition.

"If we had no religious traditions established with the city's foundation and passed down from hand to hand, it would still be clear in the present crisis that divine power has defended Rome and I should think it impossible for men to neglect religious observances. Consider the successes and failures of recent years: you will find that obedience to the gods has led to success, indifference to failure. First of all take the war with Veii: it was fought for many years, an uphill battle. It did not come to an end till we drained the Alban lake—by divine command. What about this recent disaster to our city? Did it come before we had ignored the heavenly voice telling us of the Gauls' approach, before our envoys had broken international law, before we, instead of punishing their offence, let it pass—out of this same indifference towards the gods. In consequence we were conquered, taken captive and put up for ransom; we were punished by gods and men, an example to the world. Defeat turned our thoughts to religion. We took refuge with the gods on the Capitol, in the home of Jupiter the Best and Greatest. In the collapse of our state we buried some of our holy objects in the earth, and removed others to nearby cities out of our enemies' eyes. Abandoned as we were by gods and men we did not stop worshipping the gods. Accordingly they gave us both our country and victory, and the military glory we had possessed and lost, and directed terror, rout and massacre against our enemies, who in the blindness of greed broke treaty and faith in the weighing of gold.

"Consider, gentlemen, the grave consequences in practice of honouring or neglecting divine power. Do you realise what a crime we are in danger of committing—though we have hardly escaped from the disastrous shipwreck of past offences? We possess a city founded with favourable auspices and auguries. Every corner of it is filled with the divine life of the gods. The regular sacrifices have fixed places as they have fixed dates. Gentlemen, do you propose to abandon all these gods, gods of the whole community, gods of your own family? Put your attitude alongside the behaviour of that splendid young man C. Fabius. In the recent siege he won the enemy's admiration as well as yours when he passed down from the Citadel through the armed Gauls to offer the annual sacrifice of the Gens Fabia on the Quirinal. Are you voting to maintain family cults even in wartime but to abandon the state-cults and the gods of Rome in peacetime? Do you think that the official priests should take less pains over the public observances than a private individual over the annual family-festival? Someone may suggest that we will continue our observances at Veii, or else send priests here from Veii to carry them on. Neither of these is possible without the destruction of religion. Without making a classified catalogue of all the services and all the deities, is it thinkable that at the festival of Jupiter the god's own table should not be spread on the Capitol? No need to remind you of Vesta's undying fires, of the image kept in the security of her temple as a guarantee of empire, of the shields of Mars Gradivus, of our father Quirinus. Do you propose to leave all these sacred objects on secular soil, objects that go back to the foundation of the city and even beyond?"

"Think what a difference there is between us and our predecessors! They passed on to us some ceremonies to be performed on the Alban Hill and in Lavinium. There was a tabu on transferring these ceremonies from enemy cities to Rome; can we without breaking a tabu transfer ceremonies from here to the enemy city of Veii? Remember how often ceremonies have to be repeated because through fault or accident, some detail has been omitted from the traditional ritual. After the portent of the Alban Lake, at a time when our country was engaged in war with Veii, it was simply the repetition of the ceremonies and auspices which brought us new life. More, it is in full mindfulness of the religion of our fathers that we have introduced foreign gods to Rome and established fresh gods. Juno the Queen was recently brought from Veii on to the Aventine. What a marvellous day that was! The crowds! The enthusiasm of the ladies! We have given instructions for a temple to be built to Aius Locutius in honour of the voice from heaven heard on the Via Nova. We have added the Capitoline Games to the other annual festivals, and established on the authority of the Senate a new college of priests to control it. What need was there for these new enterprises if we proposed to join the Gauls in withdrawing from the city of Rome? Did we remain in the Capitol through all those months of siege not of our own free will, but out of fear of the enemy? We are talking about ceremonies and temples. How about priests? Does the degree of your impiety ever cross your mind? There is only one place for the Vestals to live and nothing but the sack of the city has ever caused them to stir from it. There is a tabu preventing Jupiter's priest from spending even a single night outside the city. Are you going to make them into priests of Veii instead of Rome? Vesta, are your own Vestals going to abandon you? Is the Priest going to live abroad and night after night pile up the guilt for himself and his country? Almost all public business has to be transacted within the city's boundaries after taking auspices. Is this to be forgotten and ignored? The _comitia curiata_, which takes decisions about war, and the _comitia centuriata_, which elects consuls and military tribunes, can only meet in the traditional places after auspices have been taken. Are we going to transfer these to Veii? Or are the people to congregate at great inconvenience in this city, when it has been abandoned by gods and men, simply for the formal assemblies? . . .

"Here stands the Capitol where men discovered a human head, to receive divine assurance that in that place lay the head and crown of empire. Here, when the Capitol was liberated and the auguries were being taken, to the great joy of your elders, the gods of Youth and the Boundary refused to be shifted. Here are the fires of Vesta; here are the shields which came down from heaven, here are all the gods and their favour—if you stand firm."

Livy 5, 51, 4-10; 52; 54, 7.

The historical references relate quite largely to events recorded earlier in the same book. It is of course special pleading to suggest that the Romans retired to the Capitol to be under Jupiter's protection; the Capitol was their citadel. Auspices and auguries differ in that auspices are explicitly from the flight of birds, auguries are omens of any kind. The festival of Jupiter took place in the plebeian games; it was a formal senatorial banquet on the Capitol at which the statues of Jupiter, Juno and Minerva were present. Vesta was honoured in every home as goddess of the hearth, and her temple was the hearth of the whole community. The Palladium, a wooden statue of Pallas (Minerva), was kept there. A small shield was believed to have fallen from heaven in the reign of Numa as a sign of divine favour; it was guarded by the Salii, priests of Mars Gradivus ("on the March") and Quirinus ("the Mars of peace"). In his argument about new cults the worthy statesman appears to be wanting the best of all worlds. Aius Locutius is a typical example of the *Sondergötter*, the *numina*, the powers of a limited function. Similarly in the next century there was established a cult of Rediculus Tutanus, who turned Hannibal back and kept Rome safe. The religious boundary of the city (*pomerium*) is an important concept: the *comitia centuriata* (formally an organization for war) was one of the few bodies to meet outside. The *comitia* were the formal assemblies of the people for the transaction of public business. Livy comments that Camillus' words were effective, especially when he spoke about religion.

One of the most telling indications of the political importance of Roman religion may be seen in the fact that Julius Caesar, an avowed unbeliever, held the office of *pontifex maximus,* and Cicero, an avowed sceptic, held the office of augur.

So we may consider divination by means of dreams exploded with all other forms of divination. To tell the truth, superstition has

spread throughout mankind and taken advantage of human
weakness so that very few are not in its grip.

Cicero *On Divination* 2, 72.

Yet he publicly fostered that superstition.

It is worth dwelling for a little on Augustus' religious policy;
that shrewd statesman knew what he was about. Early in his reign
Horace, the former Epicurean, pleaded for a religious restoration
as essential to the political revival.

> Roman, however guiltless, you will pay the penalty
> for the sins of your fathers, until you restore the temples,
>   the broken down shrines of the gods,
>   the statues black with smoke.
> You are under heaven: to that you owe your empire.
> Everything springs from that: on that depends the future.
>   Neglect of the gods has brought
>   sorrow and disaster on Italy.

Horace *Odes* 3,4, 1-8.

The poets were following, sincerely enough no doubt, lines of
thought made clear to them by the emperor's minister Maecenas.
So Vergil centres *The Aeneid* on a religious vision, in Aeneas' descent to the underworld, and in that context proclaims Rome's
destiny.

> Others will forge the smoking bronze in lovelier lines,
> no doubt, and draw from marble lifelike looks,
> will plead cases with finer eloquence, will map out
> with ruler the movements of the sky and publish the rising of stars.
> Roman, remember your task is to rule the nations with authority
> —there lies your skill—to make a habit of peace,
> to spare the humbled and war down the proud.

Vergil *Aeneid* 6, 847-53.

Augustus has left us in the great monument at Ankara the
record of his achievements as he wanted them to be seen.

I built the Senate-house and the Chalcidicum adjoining it, the Temple of Apollo on the Palatine together with its porticoes, the Temple of the divine Julius, the Lupercal, the portico at the Circus Flaminius, which I permitted to be called the portico of Octavius after the name of the man responsible for building an earlier one on the same site, a box in the Circus Maximus, the Temples of Jupiter Feretrius and Jupiter the Thunderer on the Capitol, the Temple of Quirinus, the Temples of Minerva, Juno the Queen and Jupiter Liberty on the Aventine, the Temple of the Lares at the summit of the Sacred Way, the Temple of the Di Penates on the Velia, the Temple of Youth, and the Temple of the Great Mother on the Palatine. I restored the Capitol and the theatre of Pompey, both works involving considerable expense, without insisting on my name being attached to either. . . . In my sixth term as consul by decree of the senate I restored eighty-two temples of the gods within the city, leaving out none which at that point required restoration. In my seventh term as consul I restored the Via Flaminia from the Capitol to Ariminum and all the bridges, apart from the Mulvian and Minucian, which did not need repair. On my own personal property I used spoils of war to build a temple to Mars the Avenger and the Forum of Augustus. On ground purchased for the most part from private owners I built a theatre adjacent to the Temple of Apollo; this took the name of my son-in-law M. Marcellus. I used spoils of war to make consecrated offerings on the Capitol in the Temple of the divine Julius, the Temple of Apollo, the Temple of Vesta, and the Temple of Mars the Avenger. These cost me some hundred million sesterces.

Augustus *Res Gestae* 19-21.

The political and religious are closely intertwined in the record of this reign. The Temple of Apollo on the Palatine was his most famous foundation, begun about 36 B.C. and dedicated in 28 B.C. Julius had a temple in the Forum, dedicated on 18 Aug. 29 B.C. The Lupercal was a sacred cave on the Palatine where the she-wolf suckled Romulus and Remus according to the legend. Augustus tidied it up and turned it into a *nymphaeum*. The Temple of Jupiter Feretrius was more of a restoration, dating from 31 B.C. The Temple of Jupiter the Thunderer commemorated the emperor's escape from a thunderstorm in Spain in 26–25 B.C.; it was dedicated on 1 September 22 B.C. The temple of Quirinus on the Quirinal dated from 16 B.C. The three Aventine temples, from much the same period, were restorations. The temple of the Great Mother was a rebuilding after fire in A.D. 3, the only non-Roman foundation. The Capitol refers to the great Temple of Jupiter, Juno and Minerva, which also suffered from fire in 9 B.C. The sixth consulship was 28 B.C.; the restorations met the demands of

Horace, quoted above. The seventh consulship was 27 B.C. The temple of Mars the Avenger was vowed after Philippi; its dedication was curiously delayed till 2 B.C. The benefactions were no doubt large, but Suetonius (*Augustus* 30) records benefactions to the Capitoline Temple alone of more than this total figure, which shows how easily such figures become inflated.

The most interesting of all the religious revivals of his reign was the *Ludi Saeculares*, the festival of the Century, a ritual of purification and rebirth, supposed to take place once in the lifetime of the longest-lived citizen. Augustus held a celebration directed to national renewal in 17 B.C. It happens to be exceptionally well documented. We have the text of the Sibylline Oracle enjoining the celebration.

But when the longest span of life for men
has passed, journeying through a hundred-and-ten-year cycle,
remember, Roman, and if you should forget,
remember all this. To the immortal gods
make offering in the meadow by the copious flow of Tiber,
at the narrowest point, when night has come on the earth,
and the sun has hidden his beams. There sacrifice
to the Moirae, source of all being, lambs and goats
dark in colour, and for the Ilithyiae, placate
the protectors of birth with offerings in due ritual. To Earth
let a black sow be consecrated, pregnant with her farrow.
Let spotless white bulls be led to Zeus' altar,
by day not night. To the gods of heaven
sacrifice is made by day. So likewise make
your offering. Hera's temple must receive from your hands
a fine white cow. Phoebus Apollo too,
who bears the name of the Sun, must receive the same
offering, being Leto's son. Hymns sung in Latin
by boys and girls must echo round the temples
of the gods. The girls must have their own separate choir,
the boys' male-voice chorus be separate, but all
have their parents alive, their family tree in flower.
On that day the matrons yoked in marriage
must bow the knee by Hera's sacred altar
and invoke the goddess. Give expiatory offerings to all,
men and women, especially the women.
All must bring from home appropriate gifts

for mortals to bring from the first-fruits of their possessions,
gifts for the powers of the underworld and the blessed
gods of heaven. All these should lie in a pile
until the men and women duly seated
are ready to receive them. By day
and night without interruption, on seats fit for a god,
let all the people keep festival. Let merriment mix with solemnity.
Keep this firmly fixed in your mind:
so shall all the land of Italy, all the land of Latium
be always subject to your rod.

Sibylline Oracle in Zosimus 2, 6.

> The Sibylline books were a source of oracular wisdom kept under the care of the Fifteen, a special priesthood, and consulted only at the command of the Senate. Through the Republican period they were used at times of crisis, especially in war. The place of celebration by the Tiber was known as Tarentum and was believed to be an entry to the Underworld. Hence the black victim and the offering by night. The Moirae (Fates) and Ilithyiae (Powers of Childbirth) are Greek: Rome had been for centuries permeated with Greek culture, but Augustus knew well that half of his empire was Greek. Jupiter (the oracle being in Greek has Zeus) and Juno (Hera) have white offerings on a high altar by day. Phoebus Apollo was Augustus' patron god: he had a shrine at Actium where Augustus won his decisive victory over Antony and Cleopatra; he was, as a god of youth, light, culture and the arts of peace, peculiarly appropriate to the impression Augustus wanted to make; and his great temple on the Palatine was Augustus's greatest foundation. The banquet at the end is the sellisternium mentioned in the inscription which follows.

We have also an important though somewhat repetitive inscription giving an account of the ceremonies.

> On the following night in the meadow by the Tiber the emperor Caesar Augustus sacrificed to the Moirae nine ewe-lambs, to be wholly offered, according to the Greek ritual, and nine she-goats according to the same ritual, with the following prayer:

> "O Moirae, as is written in the Great Books for you that in every respect everything may prosper for the citizens, the people of Rome, you should receive a sacrifice of nine ewe-lambs and nine she-goats. I pray and beseech you to increase the power and authority of the citizens, the people of Rome, in war and peace, protect for ever the name of Latium, grant for all time safety, vic-

tory and might to the citizens, the people of Rome, look favourably upon the citizens, the people of Rome, and the armies of the citizens, the people of Rome, and keep safe the state of the citizens, the people of Rome; that you may look with kindly grace on the citizens, the people of Rome, on the College of Fifteen, on me, my family and household, and that you may receive this sacrifice of nine ewe-lambs and nine she-goats duly offered. For this reason accept the sacrifice of this ewe-lamb and look with kindly grace on the citizens, the people of Rome, and on me, my family and household."

On the completion of the sacrifice performances were held by night on a stage with no auditorium attached and no seats for spectators; 110 wives of free citizens, in a script presented by the Fifteen, held a *sellisternium*, with two seats provided for Juno and Diana.

On June 1 on the Capitol the emperor Caesar Augustus offered a bull in perfect condition to Jupiter the Best and Greatest, and M. Agrippa offered a second at the same place. They used the following prayer:

"Jupiter, Best and Greatest, as is written in the Great Books for you that in every respect everything may prosper for the citizens, the people of Rome, you should receive a sacrifice of this noble bull, I pray and beseech you"—the rest as previously.

At the *atalla* were Caesar, Agrippa, Scaevola, Sentius, Lollius, Asinius Gallus, Rebilus.

Next performances were given in Latin in a theatre constructed of wood in the meadow by the Tiber, and the wives of freemen gave presentations of a *sellisternium* in the same manner. The mighty performances previously presented were continued without break. A proclamation was made:

"From the Fifteen.

Since according to excellent precedent frequently exemplified in the past, in that there has been a fit occasion for public rejoicing, the resolution has been passed to reduce the period of mourning for the wives of free citizens, and since at the time of the sacred performance of traditional ritual it has been decided that the restoration of and meticulous attention to this practice is appropriate to the worship of the gods and the observance of the cult, we give notice that it is our public duty to decree a reduction in the period of mourning for women."

In addition by night the emperor Caesar Augustus made a sacrifice of nine flat cakes, nine pastry-cakes and nine cup-cakes to the divinities Ilithyia by the Tiber, using the following prayer:

"Ilithyia, as is written in the Great Books for you, that in every respect everything may prosper for the citizens, the people of Rome, you should receive a sacrifice of nine flat cakes, nine pastry-cakes and nine cup-cakes, I pray and beseech you"—the rest as previously.

On June 2 on the Capitol the emperor Augustus sacrificed a cow to Juno the Queen, and M. Agrippa offered a second at the same place, using the following prayer:

"Juno Queen, as is written in the Great Books for you, that in every respect everything may prosper for the citizens, the people of Rome, you should receive a sacrifice of a noble cow, I pray and beseech you"—the rest as previously.

The 110 married wives of free men, duly instructed . . . he spoke for them as follows:

"Juno Queen, the prosperity of the citizens, the people of Rome . . . we, the married wives of free men, on bended knee, pray you to . . . and to increase the authority of the citizens, the people of Rome, in war and peace, to protect forever the name of Latium, grant for all time safety, victory and might to the citizens, the people of Rome, look favourably upon the citizens, the people of Rome, and the armies of the citizens, the people of Rome, and keep safe the state of the citizens, the people of Rome, that you may look with kindly grace on the citizens, the people of Rome, on the College of Fifteen, and on us . . . . So we, 110 wives of freemen of the citizens, the people of Rome, on bended knee, pray and beseech you."

At the *atalla* were M. Agrippa . . . .

Performances were given as on the previous day . . . .

In addition by night the emperor Caesar Augustus made a sacrifice of a pregnant sow to Mother Earth by the Tiber, using the following prayer:

"Mother Earth, as is written in the Great Books for you, that in every respect everything may prosper for the citizens, the people of Rome, you should receive the sacrifice of a pregnant sow in perfect condition, I pray and beseech you"—the rest as previously.

The wives of freemen presented a *sellisternium* as on the previous day.

On June 3 on the Palatine, the emperor Caesar Augustus and M. Agrippa made a sacrifice of nine flat cakes, nine pastry-cakes and nine cup-cakes to Apollo and Diana, using the following prayer:

"Apollo, as is written in the Great Books for you, that in every respect everything may prosper for the citizens, the people of Rome, you should receive the sacrifice of nine flat cakes, nine pastry-cakes and nine cup-cakes, I pray and beseech you"—the rest as previously.

"Apollo, I have presented you with these flat cakes, and prayed in due form, so to this end receive the offering of these pastry-cakes, and look down with kindly favour."

So for the cup-cakes.
With the same words for Diana.

On the completion of the sacrifice a hymn was sung by twenty-seven boys, on whom the duty was laid, all with both parents living, and the same number of girls. This was repeated on the Capitol. Q. Horatius Flaccus composed the hymn.

The following members of the Fifteen were present: Caesar, M. Agrippa, Q. Lepidus, Potitus Messalla, C. Stolo, C. Scaevola, C. Sosius, C. Norbanus, M. Cocceius, M. Lollius, C. Sentius, M. Strigo, L. Arruntius, C. Asinius, M. Marcellus, D. Laelius, Q. Tubero, C. Rebitus, Messala Messallinus.

At the conclusion of the dramatic performances . . . . close to the place where sacrifice was offered on the previous nights, an auditorium and stage were constructed, turning-posts were set up and the starting-signal given for a race for four-horse chariots. Potitus Messalla gave the signal for acrobatic riders. A proclamation was made:

"From the Fifteen. We present seven days of performances in Latin in addition to the prescribed festival, in the wooden theatre by the Tiber, beginning on June 5, Greek musical shows in Pompey's theatre at 9 a.m., Greek stage plays in the theatre in the Circus Flaminius at 10 a.m."

On June 10 a proclamation was made in the following terms: "From the Fifteen. On June 12 we shall present a hunt in . . . and circus performances . . . .

On June 12 there was a preliminary procession. Boys . . . .

M. Agrippa presented chariot-racing.

For the whole celebration the Fifteen were the Emperor Caesar Augustus, M. Agrippa . . . Cn. Pompeius, C. Stolo, C. Scaevola . . . M. Marcellus . . . .

H. Dessau *Inscriptiones Latinae Selectae* 5005.

The first part of the inscription is too fragmentary to reconstruct. It begins on the night of May 31. The Great Books are the Sibylline Books. The *sellisternium* (a kind of banquet for the gods) is not mentioned in the Sibylline Oracle. The *atalla* is unknown. Ilithyia is the Greek goddess of childbirth: the oscillation between plural and singular is slightly odd. The prayer of the *matres familiae* to Juno the Queen is defective (as are the passages which follow) and it is not clear who is their spokesman, except that it is not Augustus as it lacks the formulaic references to "me, my family and household." We can trace in the ceremonies the power of the number three and its multiples. There is cathartic and purificatory ritual, invocation of the powers of destiny and rebirth, offerings to the old Capitoline deities (though the omission of Minerva is odd; Mars, however, would be inappropriate) and the new deities (though not Julius). And as with all such festivals there is a deal of junketing to keep the people happy.

In addition to these Horace's carefully scripted hymn has survived. It seems to have been sung twice, once before the temple of Apollo on the Palatine and once before the temple of Jupiter on the Capitol.

Phoebus, and Diana lady of the forests,
glowing splendour of the sky, for ever
honoured and to be honoured, grant our petition
    at this holy season
when the song of Sibyl has commanded
picked girls and blameless boys
to worship the gods who protect the Seven
    Hills, with a hymn.
Life-giving Sun, in your golden chariot you
open and close the day, being reborn different
but the same. May you never look on any spectacle
    greater than Rome!
And you, Ilithyia, gentle in preparing
birth in due season, protect our mothers,
whether we call you "Bringer of the Daylight" or
    "Goddess of Childbirth."
Guard our growing children, goddess, and give blessing

to the Fathers' edicts and the bonds of marriage
and to the law of wedlock with its promise of
    plentiful children,
that, as it passes, the cycle of the century
may bring round again the music and the contests
played on three fine days before a crowded audience,
    three memorable evenings.
You also, Fates, who prophesy truthfully
what the Powers have decreed and the outcome of history
holds unchanged, join a prosperous future
    to all that is past.
May the Earth, rich in life of plant and animal,
present Ceres with a garland of corn!
May wind and rain from Jupiter bring healthy
    growth to our harvest!
Apollo, be gentle and favourable; put away
your bow and listen to the prayers of the boys.
Lady of the Moon, queen of the constellations,
    listen to the girls.
If Rome is your care, if from Troy came
the people who settled on the coast of Etruria,
that remnant with orders to change their home and city,
    protected as they voyaged,
the people for whom Aeneas, survivor of his country,
holy and guiltless though Troy was put to the flames,
forged a path to freedom, ready to restore
    more than they'd lost—
then, you gods, grant growth in virtue to our youth,
grant tranquillity and peace to our elders,
grant to the house of Romulus prosperity, children
    and all glory!
Grant that Anchises' and Venus' far-famed line
may receive the object of their prayer and sacrifice
of white oxen, trampling enemies who resist,
    merciful to the fallen.
Already by land and sea the Parthian
shrinks from the power and armed might of Italy,
already the Scythians and Indians have dropped their arrogance
    and are asking for terms.
Already Trust, Peace, Honour, and Chastity
(come from our past) and Virtue (long neglected)
have confidence to return, and Plenty, endowed with
    a full horn, can be seen.
May Phoebus, the seer, glorious with gleaming

bow and welcome to the nine Muses,
Phoebus, who by medical science restores the body's
    wearied limbs,
if he looks with favour on the altars of the Palatine,
may he prolong the power of Rome and prosperity
of Latium for another epoch and a future
    onward and upward.
May Diana, worshipped by Aventine and Algidus,
mark the prayers of the fifteen priests,
and lend a gracious ear to the supplication
    of the children.
We carry home hope, favourable and sure,
that this is the will of Jupiter and all the gods,
we, the choir, trained to sing the praises
    of Phoebus and Diana.

Horace Carmen Saeculare

Horace does not mention Augustus explicitly, but alludes to him as one of Anchises' line. Particularly notable are the skill with which he has worked in references to much of the ceremony, the allusion to the great figure of the Sun in his chariot crowning Apollo's temple, the link with Vergil's great work (in the mention of Aeneas and the words "trampling enemies who resist, merciful to the fallen"), the introduction of personified moral values alongside the traditional gods, the way in which the last verse centres on Jupiter but leaves the final line with Apollo.

Augustus' religious revival was successful. In the next generation the historian Velleius Paterculus ends his work with an invocation of the ancient gods.

I intend to end my book with a prayer. Jupiter of the Capitol, and you, Vesta, guardian of the undying fire, and all you deities who have raised the power of the Roman dominion to the pinnacle of the world, I invoke you, in the name of the people I call upon you. Guard, preserve and protect this present state of affairs, this peace, this our emperor, and when in death he passes from his long term of duty grant him—at a date long removed from the present—successors whose shoulders are as capable of bearing stoutly the burden of world dominion as we have found his to be. Among all the citizens sustain purposes of righteousness and bring to nothing purposes of unrighteousness.

Velleius Paterculus 2, 131.

"This our emperor" is Tiberius.

It was not really till the third century A.D. that the old political religion was wearing somewhat thin. Rome had suffered grievous defeat at the hands of Persia. There the religion of Zoroaster flourished, which spoke of the battle of light against darkness, with the Sun as one of the great generals. On the eastern fringes of the Roman empire itself in Syria, the Sun was worshipped. Perhaps he would bring new vitality and power to Rome. So in A.D. 274 the soldier-emperor Aurelian established the Sun as the great god of Rome.

> He enacted many laws, laws of considerable value at that. He reorganized the priesthoods, founded the Temple of the Sun and gave it a strong College of Priests; in addition he established a fund for repairs and for staff salaries.
>
> Scriptores Historiae Augustae *The Deified Aurelian* 35, 3.

The literary sources play this move down, but the coins show that Aurelian was not just establishing an additional god, but a new Divine Overlord.

THE SUN, THE LORD OF THE ROMAN EMPIRE
H. Mattingly and E.A. Sydenham *The Roman Imperial Coinage*
Vi Aurelian 319-22.

> Coin inscriptions "To the Unconquered Sun" are common. One (like the above, from Cyzicus) shows the Sun handing the Emperor a globe; the inscription reads TO THE SUN OUR DEFENDER (*conservatori*) (353).

But the old religion dies hard, and even when the Christian empire was firmly established we still find the cultured Symmachus (second half of fifth century A.D.) pleading on political grounds for the traditional ways.

> Each has his own practices and rituals. The divine mind has assigned different cult-practices to protect different states. A genius

of destiny is apportioned to a state at its birth as a soul to an individual. Besides there is self-interest, the greatest bond between man and the gods. This is a field where reason cannot operate; the most justifiable source for belief in the gods is the memory and evidence of prosperity. If the passage of time affords religions with authority, we have a duty to preserve a faith that has lasted so many generations, and to follow our fathers' footsteps as they followed theirs to prosperity.

Let us now imagine Rome standing at my side and addressing you in these words: "Noblest of rulers, fathers of your country, show respect for my years, years to which dutiful observances have brought me. Let me enjoy the traditional ceremonies; they have never given cause for regret. Let me have life in my own way; I am free. It is this form of worship which has brought the whole world into subjection to my laws; these rites which repulsed Hannibal from my walls, and the Senones from my Capitol. Have I been preserved merely to be the object of criticism in my old age?"

Symmachus 3, 8-9.

5. Philosophical Religion

In some ways we may treat Hesiod's *Theogony* as the first step to a philosophical religion.

> First Chaos came into being, and then
> broad-breasted Earth, the eternally firm foundation of all,
> and murky Tartarus in the depths of the broad-breasted Earth,
> and Love, most handsome of all the immortal gods,
> who relaxes the body and overpowers the mind
> and wise thinking of all men and all gods.
> From Chaos Erebus and black Night emerged into being.
> Night united in love with Erebus, conceived
> and bore Aether and Day.
> Earth first bore to be her partner
> starry Heaven, to cover her on all sides
> and to be an eternally firm home for the blessed gods.
> She bore the tall Mountains, welcome haunts of goddesses,
> the Nymphs who live in the mountain-forests.
> She bore the unharvested deep, swelling in anger,
> the Sea, without sexual desire. But then
> she lay with Heaven and bore torrential Ocean,
> Coeus, Crius, Hyperion, Iapetus,
> Theia, Rhea, Right, Memory,
> gold-crowned Phoebe, desirable Tethys.
> After them Cronos was born, young, subtle,
> most dangerous of her children; and he hated his sturdy father.
>
> Hesiod *Theogony* 116-38.

Chaos is the gap, which in many primitive mythologies arises from the forcing apart of Heaven and Earth as they lie in a tight sexual embrace. Hesiod does not give this aspect of the myth, and virtually takes the gap, Earth, and the underworld below as given—together with a motive power for change, Love. It is notable that the typical myths of cosmic sexual union do not come in until Love is in being. Heaven or Ouranos is a familiar mythological figure. Ocean was to the Greeks a river flowing round the land-mass. Towards the end of the passage we are on more familiar mythological ground.

Another precursor of philosophical religion was Pherecydes of Syros (sixth century B.C.).

Pherecydes of Syros said that Zas always existed, and Chronos and Chthonie as three first principles . . . . Chronos made out of his own seed fire, wind and water . . . . These were disposed in five recesses, and from them were formed a further large family of gods, called the Divine Family of the Five Recesses.

Damascius *On First Principles* 124.

Zas is Zeus, Chronos Time and Chthonie Earth (not under her most familiar name). The recesses, a doctrine for which Pherecydes was famous, perhaps came from Babylonian Cosmology. In another version Chronos or Cronos smears two eggs with his own semen and buries them underground.

Pherecydes has his own version of the Sacred Marriage of Heaven and Earth.

They built him a large number of fine rooms. When they had finished preparing all this—the property, the maidservants, and all the other necessities—when in fact everything was ready, they celebrated the marriage. On the third day of the wedding Zas made a magnificent tapestry and embroidered on it Ge and Ogenos and Ogenos' palaces . . . . "I am honouring you with this gift in my desire that marriages be your province. Welcome as my wife." So tradition has it for the first time there was an Unveiling Ceremony. She received the tapestry from him and answered . . . .

Grenfell and Hunt *Greek Papyri* II no 11 p 23.

The weaving of the tapestry seems to be a creation-myth. Ge is earth. Ogenos is usually taken as Oceanos, the principle of water, but is

surely Ouranos. Zas and Chthonie represent the ultimate union of
sky and earth; both must be duplicated on what we can almost call
the material plane.

The initiator of the philosophical revolution was one Thales of
Miletus, whose life is dated by the eclipse of 28 May 585 B.C. Thales
asked new questions about the matter out of which the world
came into being, and the changes in the primary substance, which
he identified with water, a liquid with the possibility of solidifica-
tion and rarefaction. The question and answer were materialistic,
though not wholly so, since Water was a primal goddess in Egypt.
Thales retained a spiritual philosophy alongside his materialism,
as Aristotle testifies.

> Some people say that the life-principle intermingles with the uni-
> verse, which is perhaps why Thales said, "All things are filled
> with gods."
>
> Aristotle *On the Soul* 1, 411 a 5

> In another version he says "Everything is full of *daemons*" (i.e., divine
> spirits). The word translated "life-principle" is often rendered
> "soul."

One of the early philosophers certainly put forward a religious
way of life. This was Pythagoras of Samos who emigrated to Cro-
ton in South Italy round about 532 B.C., where he formed a religious
community. He is a shadowy figure, clearly absorbed in mathematics, clearly a mystic with a belief in the transmigration of souls.
Centuries later the Neo-Platonist Iamblichus summed up Pythagorean religion.

> I want to expound from first principles the basis for the worship of
> the gods set forth by Pythagoras and his followers. All their dis-
> tinctions of ethical right and wrong aim at conformity with the di-
> vine. This is their starting-point, and their whole way of life is
> framed with a view to following God; this is the rationale of their
> philosophy, since it is preposterous for human beings to look for
> their good from any other source than the gods—just as if in a
> country ruled by a king a man were to do homage to some subor-
> dinate official among the ordinary citizens, ignoring the king who

actually held all the power. This is the way they see mankind be-
having. For since God exists and is Lord of all, and since it is accepted that we ought to seek benefits from our overlord, and all
grant benefits to those whom they fondly love and the reverse to
those to whom they are opposed, it is obvious that we should act
in a manner pleasing to God.

Iamblichus *On the Pythagorean Way of Life* 137.

Empedocles came from Acragas in Sicily and lived in the middle of the fifth century B.C. As a philosopher he was important for
moving from the monism of Thales and his successors to a plural-
ism which eventually paved the way for atomism. In a region
where Pythagoras had propounded his religious philosophy and
mystery-cults associated with Orpheus were found, he was himself a mystic, believing in transmigration, as these fragmentary ex-
tracts from *Purifications* show:

112 Friends, who live in all parts of the great town of golden
    Acragas, up by the citadel, with minds set on good works,
    harbours of reverence to strangers, men without a trace of vice,
    greetings. I move among you all as an immortal god,
    a mortal no more, honoured as is my due,
    crowned with garlands and blooming sprays. . .

115 There is an oracle of Necessity, a decree of the gods from of old,
    everlasting and firmly sealed with broad oaths.
    When one of the spirits whose lot is long life,
    in sin has stained his dear hands with blood
    or has forsworn himself in pursuit of strife,
    then he wander thirty thousand seasons far from the blessed
        ones,
    being born through that period in all kinds of mortal shapes.
    The power of the Air drives him into the sea,
    the sea spews him out onto dry Land, the Earth
    hurls him to the bright Sun's rays, the Sun to the eddies of Air.
    One takes him from the next; all reject him.
    Of these am I now, an exile from the gods, a wanderer,
    because I trusted in the madness of strife. . .

117 In the past I have been a boy, a girl,
    a shrub, a bird, a voiceless fish in the sea. . .

118 I wept and wailed when I saw the unfamiliar place. . .

119 From what glory, from what height of blessedness,
leaving Zeus' house do I move among mankind. . .

120 We have come under this roofed cavern. . .

121   . . .the joyless land
where Murder and death and tribes of Fates,
squalid Diseases, Corruptions and Floods
roam through the darkness over the field of Doom. . .

132 Blessed is the man who has gained the riches of divine wisdom,
wretched is the man whose views of the gods are darkened. . .

133 It is not possible for us to set him before our eyes
or hold him in our hands, which is the broadest
mainroad of Persuasion to a man's heart. . .

134 For he has no human head on his shoulders,
nor two branches sprouting from his backbone,
no feet, no swift limbs, no hairy parts;
he is simply Mind, holy, ineffable,
darting with swift thoughts all through the universe. . .

136 Will you not end this ill-omened murder? don't you see
that in the blindness of your minds you are devouring one
          another?
      Empedocles *fragments* 112, 115, 117-21, 132-34, 136.

The primal sin is taking animal food, since human souls transmigrate
into animal bodies. I have not tried to arrange the fragments in the
most plausible order.

In the first chorus of Aeschylus' *Agamemnon* there is a passage
of profound theology.

Zeus, whoever he is, if this
    name pleases him to hear,
    I use it to address him.
    I have weighed each choice;
    I cannot guess the means
but Zeus, to throw for once and all this load
    of ignorance from my mind.

No, he who of old was lord,
    bursting with pride in war,
    shall have his being unknown.

His successor met
his master, and is gone.
Zeus is victor; proclaim it with understanding,
and win understanding in all.

He guided men to wisdom.
He laid down the law:
learning comes from suffering.
Sleepless we hear in our hearts the drip
of memoried pain; good sense
comes to us against our will.

The blessing of the gods is brought with violence
as they sit on their lofty thrones.

Aeschylus *Agamemnon* 160-82.

There is a divine power in the universe, call it what we will, and he
has ordained that we learn through suffering. But Aeschylus is op-
pressed by the cycle of violence: on the human scale Agamemnon—
Clytemnestra—Orestes, on the divine (in the central stanza) Ouranos—Cronos—Zeus. In this trilogy the rule of law breaks through
the human cycle of violence. In the Prometheus-trilogy he worked it
out among the gods. In the reign of Zeus wisdom supervenes on violence.

In a fragment of *The Daughters of Helios* one of the characters
puts forward a kind of pantheism.

Zeus is air, Zeus is earth, Zeus is sky,
Zeus is the universe and all that lies beyond.

Aeschylus *fragment* 70.

The first of the great rationalists was Xenophanes (sixth or
early fifth century B.C.) who commented adversely on the tendency
of human beings to make gods in their own images.

Homer and Hesiod laid at the gods' door all
that men count shameful and blameworthy,
theft, adultery and mutual deceit. . .
So mortals imagine that the gods go through birth,
wear human clothing, with a human voice and form. . .
The Africans give their gods snub noses and black skins,

> the Thracians give theirs blue eyes and red hair. . .
> If cattle or horses or lions had hands
> or could draw with their hands or make statues as men do,
> they would draw the shapes of gods and form their bodies
> respectively just like their own.
>
> Xenophanes fragments 11; 14; 16; 15.

The fifth century B.C. saw the emergence of the popular lecturers known as the sophists. On the whole their influence was in the direction of agnosticism and scepticism. A few examples will illustrate this. First, Protagoras:

> As for the gods, I have no means of knowing whether they exist or not or what they are like. There are many obstacles to such knowledge—the obscurity of the subject and the shortness of human life.
>
> Protagoras fragment 4.

Prodicus put forward a theory about the origin of the gods.

> Prodicus of Ceos said, "Our ancestors treated as gods the sun and moon, rivers and springs, and in general everything beneficial to human life precisely because it was beneficial, just as the Egyptians do with the Nile. For the same reason bread was deified as Demeter, wine as Dionysus, water as Poseidon, fire as Hephaestus and so on with other useful objects."
>
> Sextus Empiricus Against the Mathematicians 9, 18.

Thrasymachus put forward a view which challenges orthodoxy.

> The gods have no interest in human affairs or they would not have neglected justice, the most important of all forces for good among men. As it is we see that men have no use for it.
>
> Thrasymachus fragment 8.

The effect of the sophistic critique is most clearly seen in

lines put into the mouth of Sisyphus in a satyr-play by Critias,
who obtained subsequent notoriety as leader of the Thirty Dictators who tyrannized over Athens at the end of the Peloponnesian
War.

> There was a time when human life was disorganized,
> like the life of animals. Force ruled.
> There was no reward for virtue,
> no punishment for crime.
> Then, I believe, human beings invented laws
> as executioners, so that Justice might be dictator
> over all alike, and hold violence in subjection.
> Criminals were punished.
> Now the laws prevented
> open crimes of violence.
> Covert crime continued. At this point, I believe
> some ingeniously clever man first
> invented for mortals fear of the gods, to bring
> the sanction of fear on criminals, however covertly
> they might act or speak or plan.
> So he invented divinity,
> "There exists an immortal divine being,
> hearing and seeing without bodily senses, marking
> their acts with perfect wisdom, wearing a divine form,
> ready to hear all that human beings say,
> able to see all that they do.
> Though you plot a crime in silence
> the gods will know; they are
> omniscient." With sounds like these
> he introduced the most welcome of all doctrines,
> and veiled the truth in lies.
> He proposed as a home for the gods the place where
> his proposal would have the most powerful effect,
> the region from which, as he knew, terror came
> as well as succour for those in distress,
> the circumference of the sky, where he saw
> the flashing lightning and the fearful crash
> of thunder, and the star-strewn face of heaven,
> the glorious workmanship of Time, the craftsman.
> From there the blazing molten mass of the meteor falls,
> and showers of rain come down to earth.
> He instilled these fears into mankind,
> used them to establish this gorgeous myth

of a god in a worthy habitation,
and extinguished lawlessness by law.

Critias *fragment* 25.

The most famous rationalist of the day was not one of the sophists but a man named Diagoras from the island of Melos.

> Diagoras, nicknamed the atheist, came to Samothrace. A friend said to him, "You think the gods take no interest in human affairs. Look at all these votive pictures. Don't they make you realize how many people have escaped the fury of the storm and reached harbour safely as a result of their prayers?" "Of course," he replied, "because there are no pictures to show those who were wrecked and died at sea." On another occasion he was on board ship when a storm blew up. The crew were scared and in their panic told him that it was their own fault for having him on board. He pointed out plenty of other ships in difficulty on the same course, and asked whether they supposed that they all had a Diagoras on board.
>
> Cicero *On the Nature of the Gods* 3, 37, 89.

A similar spirit of scientific rationalism is found in the Hippocratic treatise on epilepsy, "the sacred disease."

> Our subject is the so-called "sacred disease." I do not myself regard it as more divine or sacred than any other disease. It has a natural cause, and is considered a divine visitation only because people do not understand it and are surprised at its unfamiliar characteristics. They continue to argue for its divine origin because of their difficulty in understanding it, and deny its divine origin by the ease with which they assume it can be cured through spells and purifying rites. But if men attribute divinity to anything they do not understand, then the number of sacred diseases will grow considerably.
>
> Hippocrates *The Sacred Disease* 1.

Euripides of all the dramatic poets was most closely in touch with advanced philosophical thought. In *The Women of Troy* he puts, out of character and context, into the mouth of Hecabe this startling prayer.

Sustainer of the earth, throned on the earth,
whoever you are, hard to discern,
Zeus, whether natural law or human intellect,
I call on you; for moving on a noiseless path
you guide all things human along ways of justice.

Euripides *The Women of Troy* 884-8.

His plays abound in attacks on orthodox religion, on priest-craft, and particularly on the Delphic Oracle. But the total impact is not of irreligion but of religious quest.

Who knows if this thing called death is really life
and life is death?
We know only that mortal men
suffer in their time of life, and after death
know no suffering and receive no evil.

Euripides *fragment* 833.

In old age he wrote *The Bacchants*, a play about religious enthu-siasm, seemingly amoral, but a formidable and genuine power with which human beings must come to terms.

Socrates (469–399 B.C.) the ugly, snub-nosed Athenian icono-clast was immeasurably revered later, though subsequent philos-ophers tended to create a Socrates in their own image. He was in many ways a rationalist, but something of a mystic as well. We may exemplify his religious stance by four passages. The first is a prayer put into his mouth by Plato.

Dear Pan, and all you other gods of this place, grant to me to be beautiful within, and grant that all my outward possessions may accord with that which is within. May I account wisdom the only riches. May I have only so much money as a man of moderation can bear.

Plato *Phaedrus* 279 B-C.

The second passage relates to a mystical voice within him, in which he placed absolute trust. We could illustrate it from Plato or Xenophon, but one of the best accounts is in Cicero.

This is just what tradition says about Socrates, just what Socrates himself often says in the books of his followers. There is a divine power which he calls *daimonion*. He always obeyed it; its instructions were always negative not positive. In fact, Socrates—and what better authority could we ask for?—answered Xenophon's request for advice about accompanying Cyrus by giving his views and adding, "This is human advice; I consider that difficult problems should be referred to Apollo. . . ." There is a story that he noticed his friend Crito with his eye bandaged and asked what was the matter. Crito replied that he'd been walking in the country; he had pushed forward a branch which sprang back and hit him in the eye. Socrates said, "You didn't listen to me when I called you back though I always use divine guidance." It was Socrates too who, during the disaster at Delium under Laches' command, was retreating with Laches. They reached a crossroads and he refused to go the same way as the others. They asked why, and he replied that the god prevented him. Those who retreated by another route fell in with a detachment of enemy cavalry. Antipater has collected a large number of stories of Socrates' miraculous divine guidance. I shall pass them over; you are familiar with them, and I do not need to remind you of them.

Cicero *On Divination* 1, 54, 122-4.

The third passage comes from the pietistic Xenophon, but there is good reason to think that it represents an authentic aspect of Socrates' thought. It is a fairly straightforward version of the Argument from Design, and might be taken from Paley or some Victorian handbook.

Don't you think that the original creator of mankind was acting with beneficial providence in endowing men with their several senses, eyes to see the visible, ears to hear the audible? What use would scents be to us without the gift of nostrils? What capacity would we have to identify sweet and dry and all those delectable flavours if we had no tongue planted in us with a capacity for discrimination? More, don't you see providence in the working of the body? Our capacity for sight is weak, so it is shut in by eyelids which open when we want to use that faculty and close in sleep. Eyelashes grow on the lids to protect our sight from the wind. Eyebrows overlay the eyes so that no drop of sweat from the head can damage them. Our faculty of hearing admits sounds of all kinds without clogging up. Again all animals have incisor-teeth for cut-

६ ० ३ ४ ४

ting, molars for grinding the food passed on from them. So too the mouth which receives and passes on the food which animals want is set near the eyes and nostrils; but what passes out from the body is unpleasant, and the passages for that are set as far as possible away from the organs of perception. All these are providently arranged; have you any doubt whether they are the product of chance or design?

Xenophon *Memorabilia* 1, 4, 5-6.

The last, very characteristic passage is also from Plato. It is the last part of Socrates' speech at his trial, after the verdict was given and sentence of death passed.

Gentlemen of the jury, you too must be optimists in face of death, and keep firmly before your minds this single truth: it is not possible for a good man to suffer any evil either in life or death; his affairs are in the hands of the gods. . . .

Now the time has come for us to go our ways, I to die, you to live. Which of us is going to a better destiny is clear to God and to him alone.

Plato *Apology* 41C-42A.

The fundamentals of Plato's own religion will be found early in *The Republic* where he proposes to censor the educational literature if its portrayal of the gods is unsatisfactory.

"Quite right," he said, "but what would be the actual rules for speaking about gods?" "Something like this," I answered. "God must always be described as he really is, whether in epic, lyric or dramatic poetry." "Surely." "And the first point is that God is genuinely good and must be spoken about as good." "Yes." "Nothing good is harmful, is it?" "No." "And what is not harmful cannot do any harm." "Quite so." "That which does no harm does no evil." "No." "And that which does no evil cannot cause any evil." "Agreed." "Well then is the good beneficient?" "Surely." "The cause then of wellbeing?" "Yes." "Then that which is good is not the cause of everything; it is the cause of things which go well, but not of evils." "That is so." "Then," I went on, "God, being good, could not be the cause of everything, as the popular view goes; so far as human beings are concerned, he is the cause of com-

Lincoln Christian College

paratively little. Good things are far less frequent than evils among us. God is the sole cause of the good, but we must look elsewhere for the causes of evil." "Quite true." "Then," I went on, "we cannot accept from Homer or any other poet unintelligent errors about the gods like saying about the two jars which

stand on the floor in Zeus' palace
full of his dowries, one of curses, one of blessings,

and that when Zeus gives people a mixed dowry

they encounter disaster at one minute, success at the next,

but that when a man receives a dowry of unmixed evil

deprivation pursues him over the lovely face of the earth.

We cannot accept that Zeus is dispenser 'alike of curses and blessings'. If anyone claims that Athene or Zeus was responsible for Pandarus breaking a sworn truce, we shall be highly critical. So with the view that Themis and Zeus brought about the quarrel in heaven, we must not let our growing youth hear Aeschylus' words

God implants guilt in human beings
when he seeks to eradicate a house.

If anybody composes a poem incorporating lines about the Sorrows of Niobe, or the House of Pelops, or the Fall of Troy, or anything of the sort, we must either censor the suggestion that these were brought about by God, or if they are attributed to God, he must create the sort of argument we are looking for, and show that God acted for justice and goodness, and their punishment was to their benefit. What we cannot allow the poet to say is that the sufferers were pitiable and God was responsible for their suffering. If he says that the wrongdoers needed punishment and were therefore pitiable, but that divine retribution benefited them, that is all right. But to say that God being good becomes the cause of evil to any man—we must fight tooth and nail to stop anyone from saying such things in his own city, if it is to be well governed, and to stop anyone, young or old, from hearing it or spreading such a legend in prose or verse. It's irreligious, inconsistent and unedifying." "I'll vote for your law," he said. "It's a good one." "Here then," I said, "is one of our legally enforced principles in describing the gods, to which orators and creative writers must conform: God is not the cause of everything, but only of good things." "And a very important principle," he said.

Plato Republic 2, 379A-380C.

The Homeric quotations are from memory and not completely ac-
curate. Plato adds two other principles, that God does not change his
form and shape, and that he does not deceive.

Towards the end of his life Plato was still advocating the en-
forcement of such principles, and more radical ones still.

> No-one believing in the existence of gods as the laws enjoin can
> possibly be guilty of his own volition of performing an impious act
> or uttering an irreligious sentiment. If he does, it is for one of three
> reasons. Either he does not believe in the existence of gods (as
> above), or, secondly, he believes that they exist but are indifferent
> to mankind, or, thirdly he believes that they can be easily won
> over by prayers and sacrifices.
>
> Plato *Laws* 10, 885B.

In this law, propounded for Plato's final ideal commonwealth, the
last clause would condemn almost all the practitioners of the traditional religions in Plato's day and since.

In some ways the highest point of Plato's mystical vision is not
God, but the Form of the Good which is not itself part of the world
of being which contains the unchanging Forms, but lies beyond
being, transcending the Forms chronologically and in terms of
value (*Republic* 6, 509B).

In *Timaeus* Plato put forward his vision of creation.

> Let us now state the reason for the creator's creating the universe
> and the world of coming-to-be. He was good, and in one who is
> good no shadow of envy ever arises over anything. His freedom
> from envy led to the desire that all should be as similar to himself
> as possible. We are entirely justified in accepting the view of men
> of wisdom that this is the basic origin of the universe and the
> world of coming-to-be. God wanted if possible everything to be
> good and nothing evil. So he took hold of all that was visible, and
> was not in a state of rest but inharmonious, disorderly motion,
> and brought order out of chaos, reckoning it better in every way.
> For one who is perfectly good there was not and is not any moral
> possibility of acting except for the best. He took thought, and
> found that of all naturally visible things, compared as whole en-

tities, nothing rational can ever yield pride of place to the irrational; further, nothing can be endowed with mind without soul. The result of his taking thought was to set mind within soul and soul within body, and so complete the design of the universe, aiming to produce a supremely good result in accordance with nature. So according to the most probable account we must say that this cosmos is a living being endowed with soul and mind, and came into being as a result of God's providence.

Plato *Timaeus* 29D-30C.

> *Timaeus* is not easy and contains a lot of outdated physics. But this is straightforward enough. The creator is not a creator in an absolute sense: he is working on pre-existing materials. These include in some sense matter, and he stamps this with the mould of the eternal Forms to produce the world we know, the world of change, of coming-to-be and passing-away.

Aristotle (384–322 B.C.) was Plato's greatest pupil. His philosophy postulated a great ladder of existence, with at the foot (as we deduce, since it is unknowable) pure matter, potentiality without any actuality, and at the top pure form, pure actuality, which is God, the eternal Prime Mover of the universe, himself unmoved.

> There is something which is in eternally unceasing motion i.e., circular motion: this is obvious alike in theory and in fact. So that the most distant heaven must be everlasting. In addition there is something which sets it in motion. Anything which both receives and causes motion is intermediate. It follows that there must be a source of motion which causes motion without receiving motion, something eternal, substance and actuality. It causes motion in the following way. The object of desire and the object of thought move without being moved. . . . The final cause . . . causes motion in the same way as the object of love moves a lover; everything else which causes motion in other things suffers motion itself. Now if a thing suffers motion it is capable of change, topological change if not substantial change. But granted that there is some substance which causes motion without experiencing motion, and which exists in a state of actuality; then this substance has no possibility of change. For the primary form of change is locomotion, and circular locomotion at that, the very motion which this substance causes. So the source of this motion is necessarily existent, and being necessarily existent is existent as good,

and thus is a first principle. "Necessary" has a variety of meanings: it is applied to a constraint contrary to natural inclination, to anything whose absence makes excellence impossible, and to things which simply cannot be otherwise.

This is the character of the first principle upon which the ultimate heaven and so the whole world of nature depend. Its life is analogous to the best we experience so briefly. It is permanently in that state (a thing impossible to us), since its actuality is a state of pleasure (this is why waking, sensation and thought are the most pleasurable present states, and hopes and memories secondary to them). Thinking is in itself directed towards that which is of itself best, and the highest form of thinking towards the highest form of good. The mind thinks itself by participation in the object of thought, for it becomes an object of thought, so that the act of thinking and the object of thought are one and the same. For that which is receptive of the object of thought, that is of substance, is mind. In the activity of grasping its object it shows its actuality. So we may say that the mind has divinity in its grasp, actuality not potentiality, and the pleasantest and best life is of active contemplation. So if God enjoys permanently the bliss we experience occasionally, that is wonderful; if a greater bliss, that is still more wonderful. These are the facts. In addition there is life. Life is the actuality of mind, and God is that actuality, and the actuality which is the pure life of God is supremely good and eternal. We assert then that God is a living being, eternal and supremely good. It follows that life and eternally continuous existence pertain to God; for that is precisely what God is.

Aristotle *Metaphysics* 12, 7, 1-9, 1072 a 19-b 31.

> The twelfth book, which deals with first philosophy or theology, has rightly been seen as the coping-stone of *Metaphysics*. The argument is not easy, as Aristotle takes for granted matters argued elsewhere in his work, e.g., that locomotion is the primary form of change, and circular motion is primary locomotion, or that thinking is the highest form of activity, or that the subject and object of perception or thought are identical in the process of actualization. The argument is also obscured by ambiguities in translation, e.g., *nous* means both mind and the process of thinking, *energeia* alike activity, actuality, and actualization. When Aristotle says that mind thinks itself he does not mean that God is engaged in self-contemplation, but in abstract thought.

Of the two great philosophies of the Hellenistic Age, the Stoic was the more obviously and pietistically religious, though inclined to pantheism. The general Stoic view is summarized by Diogenes Laertius.

> God is a living being, immortal, rational, enjoying the perfect happiness of the intellect, admitting no evil, taking providential care of the universe and everything in it. He is not of human form. He is the architect of the universe, and a kind of universal Father, in general principle and in particular relation to that part of him which permeates the whole and is known by many names connected with its several powers. They call him Dia because everything comes to be through (*dia*) him, Zeus (*Zena*) in being the cause of life (*zen*) or active in all life, Athene inasmuch as the ruling principle extends to the aether, Hera as it works through air, Hephaestus through the creative power of fire, Poseidon through water, Demeter through earth. In the same way people have given God other titles, getting hold of some particular aspect of him.
>
> Zeno says that the substance of god is the whole universe, that is the material world: so too Chrysippus in volume one of *On the Gods*, and Poseidonius in volume one of *On the Gods*. Antipater in volume seven of *On the Universe* says that his substance is in the form of air. Boethius in *On Nature* identifies the substance of God with the Planetary sphere. The term "nature" is variously used to denote the power which holds the universe together or the power of growth in the terrestrial sphere. Nature then is a self-moved system, operating in accordance with the seminal principles, bringing into being and holding together all its products at fixed seasons, and working consistently from source to outcome. Nature has as its object a combination of utility and pleasure; the analogy of human craftsmanship shows that. Chrysippus *On Fate*, Poseidonius *On Fate* vol. 2, Zeno and Boethius *On Fate* vol. 1, all maintain that everything happens as predetermined by Fate. Fate is a chain of causation which runs through all that exists. It is the Rational Principle according to which the universe progresses. Furthermore they claim that all forms of divination are valid, if there really is providential care.
>
> Diogenes Laertius 7, 147-9.

> Zeno of Citium (335-263 B.C.) a magnetic personality, was the founder of Stoicism. Chrysippus (c. 280-207 B.C.) was the great systematic thinker of the school ("If there had been no Chrysippus, there would have been no Porch"). Boethius of Sidon (second century B.C.) was an unorthodox Stoic, as evinced by his identification of God with a part rather than the whole of the material universe. Poseidonius (c.

135-50 B.C.), polymath, was a Stoic with an eclectic trend, one of the more influential figures in introducing Stoicism to the Roman world. Three important technical terms of Stoicism are the ruling principle (*hegemonikon*), the divinity in relation to the universe, in the human soul being the mind; the seminal principles (*spermatikoi logoi*), the creative power of the divine Reason; and the Rational Principle (*Logos*), a name of God, taken into Christian thinking in John 1:1, "In the beginning was the *Logos.*"

God thus is all and in all.

We understand Jupiter to be the governor and protector of the universe, the mind and spirit of the world, the lord and creator of this fabric. Every name is his. Would you call him Fate? You will not be wrong. All things depend on him; he is the cause of causes. Would you call him Providence? You will be right. His thought takes providential care that the universe may play its role by moving securely on its course. Would you call him Nature? Your language will not be inappropriate. All things are born from him, his spirit gives us life. Would you call him the Universe? You will not be in error. He himself is the All on which you are gazing; he fills his own parts, and sustains himself and all that is his.

Seneca *Scientific Investigations* 2, 45.

And in man.

Live in the company of the gods. That man does so who at no time fails to show them his soul satisfied with what has been assigned to him and fulfilling the will of the divine spirit which Zeus has given to every man to be his commander and guide, a fragment of his very self. This is the individual mind and reason.

Marcus Aurelius 5, 27.

Cleanthes (331–232 B.C.), the second head of the school, greatly fostered the impulse to religion. We have from him in verse a brief expression of faith in the destiny predetermined by Fate, and a longer hymn.

Lead me, Zeus, and you, Destiny,
wherever you decree that I shall go.

Unhesitatingly I'll follow: yet if in sin
I refuse, I shall still follow.

Cleanthes in Epictetus Handbook 53.

Seneca cites the passage, adding, "The fates lead the man who says
Yes and compel the man who says No."

Here is the hymn.

Most glorious of the immortals, God of the many names,
       Almighty, Eternal,
Zeus, ruler of Nature, steering the universe by law,
I call on you: any mortal may rightly address you.
We are your family; we bear your likeness
alone of all creatures that live and move on the earth.
For this reason I shall for ever sing your praise and hymn your
       power.
The whole universe as it circles around the earth
obeys your will and direction, and is glad to be ruled by you.
You hold in your invincible hands a mighty minister,
the forked flaming deathless thunderbolt.
Its blast makes all of Nature quiver;
you use it to direct the universal Reason, which permeates
all things, commingling with the heavenly bodies great and small.
You are supreme king forever.
Nothing happens on earth without you, God,
or in the divine sphere of aether or in the sea,
except the foolish acts of wicked men.
Yet you know too how to put the crooked straight
and organize the chaotic. You show love for the unlovely.
This is how you have fitted good and evil into a single whole,
so that one single eternal Rational Principle should extend
       through all.
Wicked men try to evade it, poor fools.
They set their hearts on possessing good things
and do not see or hear God's universal law.
If they followed that with understanding they would have the
       good life,
but in their folly they set themselves on various evil ends,
some with a divisive ambition for fame,
some whose greed for gain displaces all else,
some pursuing relaxation or the pleasures of the flesh.
It can't work out. Times change and bring very different fruits

for all their passionate search for the opposite end.
But Zeus, giver of all, dark in the clouds, brilliant in the lightning,
save mankind from the disasters of ignorance;
scatter their folly, grant them to find
sound judgement, whose support helps you to pilot the universe
       in justice.
Then we receiving honour from you will accord you honour in
       return,
perpetually hymning your works as is right
for a mortal, since human beings have no higher privilege—
or gods either—than to sing the just praise of the eternal universal
       law.

Cleanthes in Stobaeus 1, 1, 12.

One commentator summed up the hymn "How sweet the name of Logos sounds in a believer's ear!", another pointed out that it demonstrates how far natural religion can go in satisfying the cravings of the religious temper.

It may be that Epictetus (c. A.D. 55-135), a former slave, and one of the most attractive of all Stoics, had this hymn in mind when he wrote the following.

If we had understanding, ought we to do anything else, jointly and severally, than to sing hymns, bless the Deity, and tell of his benefits? Ought we not, as we dig and plough and eat, to sing this hymn to God?—"Great is God, who has given us these tools to cultivate the earth; great is God, who has given us hands, the power of swallowing, a stomach, imperceptible growth, and the power of breathing while we sleep. . . ." What else can I do, a lame old man, but sing hymns to God? If I were a nightingale, I would behave like a nightingale; if a swan, like a swan. As it is, I am a rational being, and I ought to praise God: this is my job, and I perform it. I will not desert this post as long as I am allowed to keep it—and I charge you to join in the same song.

Arrian *Discourses of Epictetus* 1, 16.

The Epicureans had a very different attitude to religion. Epicurus in his letter to Menoeceus lays down the principles of his theology.

Put into practice the things I never used to stop urging on you, regarding them as the fundamentals of right living. Begin by the faith in the existence of a living, immortal, blessed god, just as the common notion of God is engraved on the mind, and do not apply to him anything alien to his immortality or inconsistent with his blessedness, but believe about him anything which can support that blessed immortality. Gods exist; we have clear perceptual knowledge of them. But they are nothing like the man in the street imagines; he does not even hold a consistent picture of them. Impiety is not a refusal to accept the gods of the man in the street, but attributing to the gods the picture the man in the street has of them. The assertions the man in the street makes about the gods are false suppositions, not true conceptions at all. His view is that the greatest disasters—yes and the greatest blessings—are brought on the wicked by the gods. In fact the gods, familiar to everyone with their own virtues, welcome those who are like themselves and reject as alien all that is different.

Epicurus in Diogenes Laertius 10, 123-4.

> The gods of Epicurus do not directly punish or reward. They are in that sense indifferent to mankind. But emanations from them are always streaming out, and can affect for good the man who is in tune with the infinite. Further, Epicurus did recommend religious devotions, simply because it was better to be that sort of person. (It should be said that the interpretation taken of the last two sentences above is a controversial one.)

The Epicureans were called atheists. Plainly they were not so in any normal sense of the word. The Roman Epicurean Lucretius anticipates the criticism.

> I have one fear in all this. You may perhaps think
> that your first steps in philosophy are impious, that you're
> entering a course of crime. On the contrary, more frequently
> crimes of impiety are actually the fruits of religion.
> For example at Aulis the chosen commanders of the Greeks,
> leaders of the army, brutally polluted the altar
> of the Virgin Artemis with the blood of Iphigeneia.
> A ribbon was tied round her young hair;
> it streamed in equal length down either cheek.
> She saw her father standing before the altars
> in grief, the acolytes at his side concealing the knife,
> the people shedding tears to see her.

Dumb with terror she sank on her knees to the ground.
At that moment, poor girl, it could be of no help to her,
that she had been the first to accord the king the name of father.
She was picked up by the hands of the soldiers, escorted trembling
to the altars, not to fulfil the familiar
sacrament, with the marriage-hymn ringing loudly in her ears,
but to fall, tearful, an innocent victim to her father's
guilty blow at the very hour of marriage,
for the fleet to receive a blessed voyage.
Such are the evils resulting from religion.

Lucretius 1, 80-101.

In all this we must pay a tribute to Cicero (102–43 B.C.). The great orator was a man of genuine culture, though he laid no claims to being an original philosopher. During the period of Julius Caesar's sole rule he resisted the blandishments of the dictator and retired from politics, bending his immense energies to providing Rome with a kind of philosophical encyclopaedia. Cicero was himself an Academic—at this period those who professed the name of Plato were famed for their theory of knowledge which rested on probability, not on claims to absolute knowledge—there was thus a tendency to epistemological scepticism. Cicero's main interests were in ethics and religion, and these dominate his output: *On the Nature of the Gods, Conversations at Tusculum, On Divination* and other works. His method is to present and criticize in turn the views of the more dogmatic schools; he is in general utterly opposed to the Epicureans, but sympathetic to Stoic ethical concerns; but he is always notably fair in his presentation. Here, as an example, is the opening of *On the Nature of the Gods.*

There are many topics in philosophy of which we have as yet no adequate exposition, Brutus, and, as you well know, investigation into the nature of the gods is a particularly dark and difficult area. At the same time it is attractive in its relation to psychology and essential for religious discipline. Scholars hold a variety of contradictory views on the subject, and this forms a strong argument that the origin and ground of philosophy is ignorance: the Academics were very wise to withhold assent in areas where there is no certainty. What is worse than hasty judgement? What is so ill-considered, so unfitting to the weighty demeanour of a philoso-

pher, as holding views which are not true or defending without
reservation a position taken upon inadequate grounds? On this
subject the majority hold that gods exist, a probable conclusion
and one dictated by nature, but Protagoras was agnostic and
Diagoras of Melos and Theodorus of Cyrene were atheists. Fur-
thermore, those who believe in the existence of gods hold such
varied and differing views that it would be a herculean task to go
through them all in detail.

Cicero *On the Nature of the Gods* 1,1-2.

The older schools continued. Among the works attributed to
Aristotle is a treatise *On the Universe* by some anonymous follower
of his. The date is uncertain, but the first century A.D. is a reasonable hypothesis.

In general then, God stands to the universe as a captain to a ship, a
driver to a chariot, a chorus-leader to a chorus, a lawgiver to a political community, a commander-in-chief to an army—except that
with them authority involves constant activity and anxiety and
consequent weariness, while with him it involves no trouble, no
energy, no physical exhaustion. From his place in the immovable,
he sets all things in motion and keeps them in circulation, where
and how his will determines, in their various forms and natural
propensities—just as the law of the state does not move or change
but within the minds of those who observe it directs all state-
business. . . . So, we may assume, with the greater state, the universe, God is to us law, impartial, admitting no amendment or
correction, and more powerful and permanent than laws engraved
on tablets. Under his effortless, harmonious direction the whole
ordered organization of heaven and earth is governed, an organization which extends through the whole of nature to plants and
animals each in its own genus and species through the instrumency
of its peculiar genetic inheritance. . . .

God is one, but known by many names derived from all the ef-
fects he initiates. We call him [in the accusative] Zena and Dia, using the names indifferently; it is equivalent to saying that we live
(*zen*) through (*dia*) him. He is called the son of Cronos, that is Time
(*chronos*); he exists from eternity to ages to come. He is Lord of
Lightning and Thunder; Lord of the Upper Air; Lord of Thunderbolt and Rain, titles derived from rain and thunderbolts and the
rest. Similarly he is called Lord of the Harvest, City-God, Lord of
the Family, Household-God, Lord of the Clan, Ancestral God, be-

cause of his association with these things, Lord of Society and Friendship and Hospitality, of Battle and Victory, of Purification and Retribution, God of Suppliants, God of Grace (as the poets put it); he is the true Saviour and Liberator, in short the God of Heaven and the Lower World; he takes his titles from every being and event in nature, since he is the cause of all. *The Hymns of Orpheus* puts it well:

> Zeus the first, Zeus the last, the Lord of the Lightning,
> Zeus the head, Zeus the centre, the source of all being,
> Zeus the stay of the earth and the starry sky,
> Zeus the male, Zeus the immortal maiden,
> Zeus the breath of all things, Zeus the surge of unquenchable fire,
> Zeus the root of the ocean, Zeus the sun and the moon,
> Zeus the King, Zeus the ruler of all, the Lord of the Lightning.
> He hid all men and brought them back to the joys of the light
> in the holiness of his heart, working miracles.

> I suppose Necessity (*Ananke*) is another name for him in his capacity of indefeasible (*aniketon*) cause, Destiny (*Heimarmene*) because he fastens (*eirein*) all together and moves without difficulty, Fate (*Pepromene*) because everything is finite (*peperatosthai*) and nothing in the world is infinite, Moira from the principle of apportionment, Nemesis from the different disposition (*dianemesis*) to each, Adrasteia as a cause naturally inevitable (*anapodrastos*), Aisa as an eternal (*aei ousa*) cause. . . .
> Anon (Pseudo-Aristotle) *On the Universe* 400 a 6-401b 14.

Philo was an Alexandrian Jew who sought to bring together the Hebrew scriptures and the insights of Greek philosophy into a single system. To this end he had recourse to allegorical interpretation. His treatise *Who is the Heir of Divine Things?* takes the form of an extended commentary on Genesis 15, 2-18, the story of God's promise to Abraham. It contains a fine exposition of philosophical mysticism.

> Then who is to be heir? Not the mind which is content to remain within the prison of the body, but the mind which is freed from its fetters and liberated, which has emerged outside the prison wall, which so to speak, has left itself behind. The words are "He who comes out of you shall be your heir." My soul, if you feel within

you any sort of longing to inherit the good things of God, do not merely leave behind your "land" (your body), your "family" (the senses), your "father's house" (your way of thinking); escape from yourself, come out of yourself, like the inspired corybants be filled with God just as the prophets received the touch of God. When a man's mind is inspired by God and no longer contained within itself but driven mad by yearning for heaven, led on by true reality and drawn upwards to true reality, when truth goes in front of him removing obstacles from his path and turning it into a highway—that man is the heir. Come along, mind, tell us how you migrated from your old home. You are always teaching those who have been trained to listen to the voice of the mind, saying "I migrated from the body when I had come to disregard the flesh. I migrated from the senses when I came to realize that all the objects of sense bore no relationship to truth, and to condemn their standards of judgement as illegitimate, corrupt and chockfull of false opinion and the judgements themselves as designed to enchant and deceive, ravishing truth away from the central point in nature. I migrated from my way of thinking when I condemned its irrationality for all its high and mighty opinion of itself. What colossal audacity to try to show me substances by means of shadow and facts by means of words! It can't be done. And yet it kept talking, slipping about and drifting around, unable to give a clear account of the particular qualities of underlying substances because of the ambiguities of language. Like an inexperienced child I learned from experience that it was better to abandon all these, and offer the powers of each to God, who gives the body its physical form, equips the senses for sense-perception and extends to thought the power of expression." Well, mind, you have left the others behind. Leave yourself behind in the same way. What does this mean? Do not store away for yourself the powers of thought, intelligence and apprehension, but bring them as an offering to the One in whose keeping are the gifts of precise thought and correct apprehension.

Philo *Who is the Heir?* 14, 68-74.

Finally, we may cite five broadly Platonic passages from the Roman empire on different aspects of religion. First from Dio Chrysostom (c. A.D. 40-115), a man of culture who in exile acquired a sympathetic understanding of the Cynic philosophy. He is discussing sources of religious belief.

I was suggesting that the primary source for belief in God lies in this notion which is innate in all mankind, and which arises from the facts of reality, a notion not incoherent or casual, but strong and universal throughout history, arising and persisting in every country, a general common feature of rational beings. I suggest as a second source the notion which is acquired at second hand in the mind through stories, myths and practices, some of them put into writing by well-known authors, others anonymous oral traditions. There are two sides to this belief, one a free response to religious discourse, the other a legally enforced response to prescriptive legislation: the first comes from poets, the second from politicians. Neither of these would have taken effect had the primary source for belief not been underlying them.

Dio Chrysostom 12, 39-40.

The analysis comes from Plato *Phaedrus* 237 D.

Maximus of Tyre, of whom we know little except that he lived at Rome in the second century A.D., professed the philosophy of Plato, and was a pietistic sermonizer, defends the use of images.

The divine nature has no need of images or statues; it is humanity in its weakness and distance from the divine, "as the heaven is far above the earth," which has devised these symbols, including the names of the gods and legends about them. Those who have strong powers of Recollection and can reach in the spirit straight to heaven and encounter the divine may not need images. Such a type is rare among mankind; you would never find any large group of people with such a power to recollect the divine without the help of some such support. It is like teaching children to write. Teachers have a scheme of producing faint impressions of the letters for them so that they may direct their hand along these until by the use of recollection practice makes perfect. My view is that the legislators treated mankind like a class of children and invented images for them as symbols of the reverence due to divinity, a kind of guidance of the hand, a direction towards Recollection.

Maximus of Tyre 2, 2.

The passage contains the Platonic doctrine that we have known reality before birth but forgotten it, and that all knowledge is Recollection of what we have once known.

Plotinus (A.D. 205–70) was the founder of Neo-Platonism and one of the greatest of all mystic philosophers. In this passage he describes his own mystical experience.

> On many occasions I have been lifted out of the body into my true self. I have come to be outside all other things, but within my self. I have looked on a marvellous beauty. I have then even believed myself part of a greater order. I have experienced in practice the highest life. I have reached the point of identity with the divine, I have been established within it, by reaching that state of actual being I have established myself above all the rest of the spiritual world. But after this period of remaining in the divine, I fall from spiritual understanding to reasoning, and do not understand the reason for my present descent or how my soul has come to be within my body when, even while, within the body, it has revealed its true nature.
>
> Plotinus *Enneads* 4, 8, 1.

The Neo-Platonist Iamblichus gives a philosophical account of prayer.

> Prayer is an important part of sacrificial ritual: it completes it, gives it efficacy, brings the whole operation to fulfilment. Indeed it sets a seal on all religion. It weaves an indissoluble tie of sacred communion with the gods. So I shall say a little about it. The subject is one intrinsically worthy of study, and fills a gap in our theological knowledge. I maintain that the first form of prayer is unifying; it produces contact with the divine and recognition of the divine. The second form secures the harmony of communion, and elicits gifts from the gods which complete their work before we have spoken or even thought of them. The culmination of prayer is ineffable union; its whole authority depends on the gods, and it sets our soul firmly and finally in their midst.
>
> These are the three types of prayer and they cover all religion. Prayer puts us in a state of harmonious fellowship with the gods; it also accords us blessings from the gods, of three kinds, leading to illumination, guidance in action, and utter absorption in the Divine Fire. Sometimes prayer precedes sacrifice, sometimes it is an integral part of sacrificial ritual, sometimes it is the final part of the ceremony.
>
> No religious ritual takes place without petitionary prayer. A long

period spent in prayer is food for our spirit, and opens a wider space in our soul for the gods to enter, reveals the world of the gods to human beings, makes us accustomed to the flashing beams of Divine Light, gradually perfects our inward self for contact with the gods, till it leads us to the very summit, gently abolishes our old habit of thought, implants in us the ways of the gods, arouses in us faith, fellowship and indissoluble communion, increases the divine love, kindles what is divine in the soul, purifies the soul of all that is not divine, throws away all thought of physical sex from within a spirit illuminated and of the divine aether, brings to fruition good hope and faith in the Light. To sum up, prayer turns those who use it, if I may so put it, into companions of the gods.

Iamblichus On the Mysteries 5, 26.

Alongside this we may put some words in justification of sacrifice by Sallustius, friend of the emperor Julian.

I think it worth adding a paragraph about sacrifices. In the first place, everything we have comes from the gods. It is right to give the first fruits of a gift back to the giver. So we make representative offerings, votive offerings for our property, a lock of hair for our physical selves, sacrifices for the gift of life. Secondly, prayers divorced from sacrifices are mere words. The sacrifices give life to the words. The words realize the potentiality of the life offered, the life offered gives vitality to the words. Next, everything finds its happiness in its own peculiar fulfilment, and that is its union with its first cause. This is why we pray for union with the gods. The highest life is the life of the gods, but human life is life of a sort which yearns for union with the true life. But it needs an intermediary (extremes cannot be united without a middle term) and the intermediary must be like the things to be united. The intermediary between life and life has to be life. This is why the most religious men today, as in the past, sacrifice animals, not all identically, but with an appropriateness to the particular god, and a complex ritual besides. That is enough on sacrifice.

Sallustius On the Gods 16.

6. Fears and Needs

The temples were a symbol of stability and permanence, and of a divine dimension of life. In need, fear, desperation, the individual would be likely to turn elsewhere.

To oracles for example; we have a number of lead tablets dating from the fifth to the second century B.C. recording questions put to the oracle of Zeus and Dione at Dodona. It will be noticed that though there are political consultations, notably the rueful request from Corcyra (which does date from the terrible civil strife of the fifth century B.C.) they are mostly from private individuals about business or domestic concerns.

> God. Good fortune. The people of Corcyra communicate to Zeus Naos and Dione their desire to know which god or hero they should invoke and honour with sacrifice to ensure the blessings of concord.

> The commonwealth of . . . ask Zeus Naos and Dione whether it is safe for them to join politically with the Molossi.

> Gods. Good Fortune. Evandros and his wife communicate the request to Zeus Naos and Dione. Which god, hero or spirit should they invoke with prayer and honour with sacrifice to secure present and permanent prosperity for themselves and their household? [Answer] Evandros.

> Would it be good and profitable for me to purchase for myself the house in the town and the plot of ground?

God. Good Fortune. Antiochus asks Zeus and Dione about his own health and that of his father and sister. Which god or hero is it best and most valuable to honour? [Answer] He should go quickly to Hermio.

Cleütas asks Zeus and Dione if there is profit for him in rearing sheep. [Answer] From rearing sheep.

Good Fortune. Shall I meet success as a merchant if I follow my own flair for gain, decide on my own course, and use my navigational skills?

Lysanias asks Zeus Naios and Dione whether the child Annyla is carrying is his or not.

Agis asks Zeus Naos and Dione about the blankets and pillows which . . . has lost. Could they have been taken by an outside burglar? [Answer] Agis.

> C. Michel *Recueil d'Inscriptions Grecques* 843-51.

Hermio is presumably Hermes, but may be deliberately ambiguous. Some of the other answers are not wholly clear.

Even better known than Dodona was Delphi. We think of the great political consultations, but there must have been numerous private consultations on simpler matters. In Euripides's play *Ion*, the scene is set in front of the temple at Delphi. The exchange between Ion and Creusa shows casually what might be expected.

ION: Have you come to the oracle alone or with your husband?
CREUSA: With him. He stopped at Trophonius's shrine.
ION: As a sightseer or to consult the oracle?
CREUSA: To ask him and Phoebus the same question.
ION: About crops or children?

> Euripides *Ion* 299-303.

We have a valuable body of evidence about Delphi from Plutarch, who lived not far away at Chaeronea and held a life priesthood from A.D. 95. Three of his essays, *The E at Delphi*, *The Priestess at Delphi No Longer Delivers Verse Oracles*, and *The Decay of Oracles* are a full discussion of various aspects of the oracle. Plutarch's evidence however comes from a late period, and needs to be checked against archaeological and other evidence. For example, he attributes the inspired ecstasy of the priestess to mephitic vapours from the ground. Archaeology has shown no trace of a chasm from which these might emerge, but the authorities evidently did nothing to dispel the story. Plutarch's account throws light on the actual practice of the oracle.

> We do not deprive prophecy of any basis in God or reason, when we assign a human soul as its material cause and mephitic vapour as its instrument or plectrum. In the first place the earth which generates the vapours and the sun which equips the earth with the potentiality of constitution and transmutation are traditionally among our gods. In the second place, it would not seem irrational or impossible to leave spiritual powers as superintendents, patrolmen and protectors of this constitution, slackening or tautening it at need, eliminating an excess of ecstatic distraction, and mixing in an element which can stir the soul of the subject without causing pain or damange. We do nothing contrary to this principle of rationality when we sacrifice first, crown the sacrificial victims with flowers and pour libations over them. The priests and religious officials claim that they sacrifice the victims, pour libations over their heads and observe their shivering movements as a demonstration that the god is ready to prophesy. The sacrificial offering must be pure, innocent and incorrupt in soul and body. Evidence relating to the body is easy enough to see with the eye. They test the soul by putting barley in front of the bulls and chick-peas in front of the boars. If they do not eat they are regarded as having something wrong with them. But with the goat cold water is an adequate test. A soul in its natural state could not remain indifferent or immobile in face of a shower of water. Even if it were a firm conclusion that the movement is evidence of the god's readiness to prophesy, and the failure to move of his unreadiness, I cannot see that this creates any difficulty for my position. Every faculty gives better or worse results at different moments. We may get the moment wrong; it is reasonable for the god to produce evidence.
>
> I think that the vapours are not always of the same quality, but are more or less intense at different times. As witnesses I call a great many visitors and the whole temple staff. The room in which they place those who have come to consult the god is sometimes filled with fragrant air. This does not happen frequently or regularly, but from time to time as it occurs. It is like the scent of the richest and sweetest perfumes, and it has as its source the inner sanctuary. It is presumably a kind of efflorescence produced by

heat or some other internal force. If this seems implausible, you will admit that the Pythia herself receives different impulses at different times in the inspired part of her soul, and her soul's constitution is not single and simple like that of a musical instrument which once tuned is kept at the same pitch. Many distractions take hold of her body and affect her soul; she is aware of some, unconscious of rather more. When these are dominating her, it is better for her not to enter the sanctuary and surrender herself to the god, in view of the fact that she is not undistracted, not like a well-tuned musical instrument, but in a state of emotional instability. . . .

Whenever the faculty of imagination and prophecy is properly attuned to the constitution of the spirit as to a drug, there cannot but be divine inspiration in those who utter prophecies. In other circumstances there cannot be inspiration, or the inspiration is not pure and effective but misleading, as we can see in the recent death of the Pythia. A delegation arrived from overseas to consult the oracle. Reports say that the sacrificial victim remained unmoved and impassive through the initial libations, but in their anxiety for the reputation of the oracle the priests went too far; they kept at it until the victim, soaked to the skin and practically drowned, eventually gave in. What did this involve for the priestess? According to the report she went down to the oracular chamber reluctantly and unenthusiastically. In her first answers it was clear from the hoarseness of her voice that there was something wrong with her responses. She was like a ship in a storm. She was filled with an evil spirit which was inhibiting her. Finally she showed signs of complete distraction. She gave a fearful, unintelligible scream, dashed to the door, and flung herself out. The deputation ran away; so did Nicander, the interpreter, and the other religious representatives present. Before long they went back in, and picked her up. She was still conscious but died a few days later.

For the same reasons they insist on the Pythia keeping her body pure from sexual intercourse, and her life in general free from contact and communication with strangers. They take the omens before oracular responses are given, trusting the god to show whether her constitution and disposition are in a fit state to experience divine inspiration without harm. The power of the spirit does not affect everyone in the same way, or the same people in the same way on every occasion. As I have been suggesting, it provides a kind of starting-point, a spark to light the flame for those who are in a fit condition to go through the transforming experience. The power comes from gods and divine spirits. Even so it is not inexhaustible; it is subject to deterioration with the passage of time; it does not extend into that eternity which wears out all that exists between the earth and the moon according to our philosophy.

Plutarch *Moralia* 436E-437D, 438A-D.

> The Pythia is the priestess of Apollo at Delphi who, in a state of ecstasy, however induced, uttered oracular responses, which the interpreter put into plain (or ambiguous) Greek, in classical times, in verse-form. There is a reasonable supposition that the oracle had an efficient intelligence service, and was able from gathered wisdom to give generally sound advice. Plutarch's philosophy was a form of Platonism.

Delphi and Dodona were by no means the only oracles in the Greek world. Apollo had another famous oracle at Didyma in Asia Minor. The passage from Euripides' *Ion* mentions the oracle of Trophonius at Livvadhia, not very far from Delphi. We have from Pausanias a valuable account of the process of consultation.

> Here is an account of the oracle. When a man decides to make his descent to Trophonius' oracle, he first spends a specified number of days in a building dedicated to the Good Spirit and Good Fortune. During his period there he has to observe various purificatory rules, including abstinence from hot baths, washing in the river Hercyna. He has ample meat from the sacrifices, for anyone making a descent offers sacrifice to Trophonius and his children, to Apollo, Cronos, Zeus under the title of the King, Hera the Charioteer, and Demeter with the title Europe, Trophonius' supposed nurse. At each sacrifice there is a diviner present who inspects the victim's entrails and as a result of the inspection declares to the man making the descent whether Trophonius will accord him a kindly and favourable welcome. Beyond the entrails of all other sacrificial victims Trophonius' will is revealed by a ram sacrificed over a pit on the very night of the descent, with an invocation of Agamedes. All the earlier sacrifices may have appeared propitious, but they go for nothing unless the entrails of this ram carry the same message, but if they accord with the other, then the inquirer can make his descent in a spirit of hopefulness, and this is what he does.

> First he is escorted by night to the river Hercyna by two thirteen-year-old sons of citizens, each known as "Hermes," who proceed in person to anoint him with oil and wash him, and per-

form all the other duties of attendants. From there he is escorted by the priest, not immediately to the oracle, but to two springs situated close to one another. From these he drinks "the water of Forgetfulness" in order to forget all that was occupying his mind, and afterwards the water of Memory which enables him to remember all that he has seen in the course of his descent. Next he is allowed to view an image supposedly carved by Daedalus—the priests show it only to those who are going to consult Trophonius. He gazes at it, offers worship and prayer. Now he makes his way to the oracle, wearing a linen tunic tied with ribbons, and the local shoes on his feet. The oracle is outside the grove on the mountainside. It is surrounded by a circular base of white marble, of height just under two cubits and circumference much that of a small threshing-floor. Set into these foundations stand two vertical posts, made of bronze, as are the cross-pieces which link them together; between them gates have been constructed. Inside the precinct is a cavern in the ground, not natural, but scientifically constructed on strict architectural principles. In shape this building is like a bread-oven, at a guess measuring about six feet by not more than twelve at most in depth. There is no structural means of descent to the bottom. But when a man comes to consult Trophonius they fetch him a light narrow ladder. On descending, he finds a gap between the building and the floor, apparently about a foot and a half wide and rather less than one in height. The man who is making the descent lies flat on the floor holding barley-cakes kneaded with honey in his hands, and pushes his feet through this gap, moving his whole body forward and making an effort to get his knees into the aperture. Then the rest of his body is suddenly jerked forward after his knees, rather as a large swift-flowing river can catch a man in its current and pull him under. He is now within the shrine. There are a variety of ways for communicating the future to him, some through speech, some through spectacle. Those who have made the descent return to the upper world through the same aperture feet first. . . . After his return from Trophonius' shrine he is again escorted by the priests who sit him down on a chair called the Chair of Memory not far from the shrine, and while he is seated there ask him what he has seen and learned. When he has told they hand him over to his own family. By now he is paralysed with fear and does not recognize himself or any of those around him. They take him up and carry him to the hostel where he was staying before under the care of Good Fortune and the Good Spirit. Later his power of laughter and his other faculties will return unimpaired. I am not writing at second hand. I have seen other applicants; I have consulted Trophonius myself. Those who make the descent to Trophonius' shrine have to dedicate a tablet inscribed with an account of the words or spectacle revealed to them.

Pausanias 9 (Boeotia) 39, 5-14.

We have also a number of questions to an oracle in Egypt ranging over some centuries. Here is one from the first century A.D.

> My Lord Sarapis, the Sun, my Benefactor. Is it right that my son Phanias and his wife should refuse to enter into agreement with his father, and should contradict him and not offer a contract? Give me an answer which agrees. Goodbye.
>
> *Papyrus Oxyrhynchus* 1148.
>
>> There is a kind of pun in the word "agrees": "agrees with the truth," but also "recommends agreement."

From the second century A.D.

> To Zeus the Sun, Almighty Serapis and his fellow-gods. Nike wants to know whether it is profitable for me to buy from Tasarapion her place Sarapion also called Gaïon. Grant me this.
>
> *Papyrus Oxyrhynchus* 1149.

From somewhat later, about A.D. 300, we have a whole string of questions, which reflect the deteriorating economic situation.

72. Shall I receive the gratuity?
73. Shall I remain in the place where I have been posted?
74. Am I going to be sold?
75. Am I going to make any profit from my partner?
76. Am I permitted to make a deal with the other man?
77. Am I to be reconciled with my son?
78. Am I to get leave?
79. Shall I receive the money?
80. Is he alive overseas?
81. Is it going to be a profitable operation?
82. Are my goods to be distrained?
83. Shall I find a buyer?

84. Am I able to bring off what I have in mind?
85. Am I to end up in the gutter?
86. Shall I become a refugee?
87. Shall I be appointed ambassador?
88. Am I to be appointed to the Council?
89. Is my escape to be intercepted?
90. Am I going to get a divorce from my wife?
91. Have I been poisoned?
92. Am I going to get my rights?

Papyrus Oxyrhynchus 1477.

The questions come from varying sources, slave and free, men of eminence and humble folk. The questions about high office do not arise from ambition; at this point in history high office was a grave financial liability.

Augury and divination in various forms were a sign of similar insecurity. Cicero wrote a treatise on the subject, drawing on Greek sources, and packed with anecdotes. As a sceptic he rejects the claims of divination, but acknowledges their magnetic power.

There is a long-standing view which can be traced back to the age of myth and which holds its place by the unanimous assent of the people of Rome and of every other nation, that there is among human beings some kind of power of divination. The Greeks call it prophecy or the foreknowledge and understanding of future events. What a magnificent blessing, leading us as close as human nature can attain to the power of the gods—if it really exists. We do many things better than the Greeks, not least the name we give to this exalted faculty, derived from the divine; the Greeks, in Plato's interpretation, call it after madness.

Cicero *On Divination* 1, 1.

The Latin *divinatio* comes from *divi* "gods"; Plato *Phaedrus* 244C derives the Greek *mantike* from *manike* (the same root as our "mania").

Those in need of healing would be likely, especially in the Hellenistic and Roman periods when the cult became prominent, to go to one of the great hospital shrines of the healing-god Asclepius, at Epidaurus or Cos or Pergamum. Other centres were at Tricca in

Thessaly, where the cult may have had its origin, at Athens, at Titane and Gerenia in southern Greece, at Balagrae near Cyrene in North Africa, at Lebene in Crete, at Smyrna, and at Rome where the god was Latinized as Aesculapius and housed on the island in the Tiber where the hospital of S. Bartolemeo still stands. We have a remarkable testament of personal devotion to Asclepius in the writings of the hypochondriac Aelius Aristides. Even more interesting are the records of temple-cures from Epidaurus.

God. Good Fortune. Healings of Apollo and Asclepius.

Cleo was pregnant for five years.

She had been pregnant for five years, went in supplication to the god and slept in the sanctuary. Immediately after leaving, once outside the precincts she bore a son, who immediately after birth washed in the spring and went round with his mother. In her good fortune she had inscribed on her thank-offering: "Do not wonder at the size of this tablet, but at the greatness of the god. Cleo bore in her womb the burden for five years, slept in the sanctuary and was made whole. . . ."

Ambrosia from Athens, blind in one eye.

She came in supplication to the god, but as she walked round the temple she laughed at some of the cures as implausible or impossible, with the lame or blind restored to health by seeing a vision in sleep. She slept in the sanctuary and saw a vision. She thought the god stood over her and said that he would make her well, but she must present a silver pig as a thank-offering to the temple, as a record of her ignorance. With these words he made an incision in her diseased eye and poured in a salve. When day broke she came out cured. . . .

Euphanes, a boy from Epidaurus.

He was suffering from gallstones and slept in the sanctuary. He thought the god stood over him and said "What will you give me if I cure you?" He answered "Ten knucklebones." The god laughed and promised to help him. When day broke he came out cured.

W. Dittenberger *Sylloge*[3] 1168.

From these and similar records it is clear that the priests were skilled in surgery and pharmacology, and used drugs or hypnotism to present a divine epiphany by night and, if necessary, apply treatment.

The records show much wisdom from the priests and genuine religious faith from the patients.

The borderline between magic and religion is not an easy one to draw. Basically religious petition depends on the independent will of supernatural beings, whereas magic is compulsive. In pure magic the result is bound to ensue, provided that every part of the ritual has been precisely carried through, and that it is not counteracted by a more powerful magic. But the two interact. What are plainly religious invocations have to be performed with meticulous accuracy; what are plainly magical spells contain invocations of supernatural beings.

The miscellaneous encyclopaedist, the elder Pliny, records numbers of magical cures. Here is one.

A cure for toothache. Stand under an open sky on the living earth with shoes on. Grasp the head of a frog. Open his mouth and spit into it, ask him to take away the toothache and then let him go alive. To be done on a day and at an hour of good omen.

Pliny the Elder *Natural History* 28, 23.

The open sky gives contact with the heavenly gods. Transference of a hurt to something else is a common magical formula; it underlies the Hebrew ritual of the scapegoat. The frog is a creature of earth and water. So by wearing shoes you separate yourself from the soft earth which might bring the toothache back.

We have seen similar magical recipes in Cato's treatise *On Agriculture*. Petronius has an account of a magical cure for impotence.

I took a brief stroll and settled down where I had been the previous day. Presently Chrysis came into the arbour with an old woman trailing after her. She embraced me and said: "Well, my fine fellow, are you in better form today?" The old woman produced a skein of multi-coloured threads and wound it round my neck. She spat in some dust, and made a mixture, placed it on her middle finger and marked my forehead with it, although I tried to stop her. . . . When she had completed her spell, she told me to spit three times, and, again three times, to drop into my crotch some pebbles which she had magicked and wrapped in purple. Then

she reached in with her hands and began to test my virility. Before
you could say "knife," the nerves responded to her command,
they twitched and swelled till they filled the old woman's hands.
She was delighted and called out "Look, Chrysis, look, what a
hare I've started for others to hunt!"

Petronius *Satyricon* 131.

> The gap in the narrative is due to a defective manuscript: we do not
> know what other spells there were if any. Bright colours are used for
> healing and love magic, dark for black magic. Three, the first odd
> number, is always powerful, spitting is apotropaic, but spittle is also
> therapeutic. The power of sex was believed to reside in the hand. The
> pebbles were no doubt phallic in shape and firm in texture, wrapped
> to retain their magical potency.

We have a number of literary descriptions of magic. One of the
finest, finely dramatized, is an account of a love-spell in Theocritus.

Where are my laurel-leaves? Come along, Thestylis. Where are
my love-charms?
Garland the bowl with the crimson flower of wool;
I'll charm my cruel lover back with fire-magic—
it's twelve days since the wretch came near me;
he doesn't know whether I'm alive or dead;
he's not even knocked at my door, damn him! I expect
Eros and Aphrodite have gone taking his swift fancy elsewhere.
Tomorrow I'll go to Timagetus' wrestling-ground
to see him and confront him with what he's doing to me.
For now, I'll magick him with the fire-spell. Moon,
shine bright. I will sing to you, goddess, under my breath
to Hecate below, who makes even the dogs shiver
as she passes among the graves and dark blood of the dead.
Welcome, dread Hecate, be with me to the end,
and make these spells of mine as potent as Circe's,
or Medea's, or Perimede's of the golden hair.
      Wryneck, draw my lover home.
Barley-meal on the fire first. Thestylis,
throw it on. Idiot, where have your wits flown?
Have I become a scorn to a filthy beast like you?
Throw it on, saying, "These are Delphis' bones I'm throwing on."
      Wryneck, draw my lover home.
Delphis caused my pain. Against Delphis I set fire to
this laurel, and as it crackles loudly, and suddenly

catches and burns away to invisible ash,
so may Delphis' flesh waste in the fire of love.
     Wryneck, draw my lover home.
As I melt this image with divine favour,
so may Delphis of Myndos be melted with love.
As this bronze wheel turns by Aphrodite's grace,
so may he turn and turn before my door.
     Wryneck, draw my lover home.
Now to burn the bran. Artemis, you can move
the adamantine gates of Hades, and all else unshakeable,
Thestylis, the dogs are barking all through the city.
The goddess is at the cross-roads. Quick, sound the bull-roarer.
     Wryneck, draw my lover home.
Now the sea is silent, the winds are silent,
but the ache within my heart is never silent.
I am all on fire for the man who has made me
in my misery neither virgin nor wife.
     Wryneck, draw my lover home.
Three times I pour this libation, Lady, three times say this prayer.
Whether his bedfellow be woman or man,
let them be forgotten, as legend says that Theseus once
forgot on Dia Ariadne of the lovely hair.
     Wryneck, draw my lover home.
The coltsfoot grows in Arcadia, a plant which drives
all the fillies and mares galloping madly through the mountains.
So let me see Delphis coming to my door
from the oil of the wrestling-ground, like one driven mad.
     Wryneck, draw my lover home.
Delphis lost this tassel from his cloak.
I pluck it to shreds and throw it to the fire to consume.
Ah, ineluctable Love, why have you fastened on to me,
like a leech from the swamp, sucking all the dark blood from
              my flesh?
     Wryneck, draw my lover home.
To-morrow I'll squeeze the juice from a lizard and make a potion.
For the moment, Thestylis, take this mixture and smear it
over his doorway, while the night still lasts,
spit and say: "I am smearing Delphis' bones."
     Wryneck, draw my lover home.

                              Theocritus *Idylls* 2, 1-63.

Hecate is goddess of the underworld and goddess of witches, worshipped at crossroads. Circe, Medea and Perimede (or Agamede) were all noted witches. The wryneck is a bird, whose curious neck-movements may have seemed supernatural; it is fastened to a wheel and then spun round to bind the charm fast. The word may be applied to the wheel without the bird. The barley-meal, laurel and wax image are all surrogates for Delphis. Bran is known elsewhere as binding magical rites. The number three is again prominent. Magic which uses a piece of the victim's clothes, or is applied to his house is common enough. Most of the magic is straight-forward sympathetic magic: as to A, so to B. The word lizard is also used of the male sex-organ; there is a kind of *double entendre* about the magic. Thestylis is to spit so as to avert the spell from herself. Other apotropaic elements earlier include the crimson wool and the sound of the bull-roarer.

We have also a poem of dedication of such a magic wheel.

> Nico's wheel which knows how to bring a man
> from overseas, boys from their rooms,
> ornamented with gold, carved of clear amethyst,
> is dedicated as a cherished gift, Aphrodite,
> hanging from a soft thread of crimson wool,
> the Thessalian witch's offering.
>
> Anon in *Greek Anthology* 5, 205.

A fragment of a mime of Sophron shows a magic ritual.

> . . . set down the table
> as it is. Take a lump
> of salt in your hand,
> laurel behind your ear.
> Go to the hearth.
> Sit you down. Give me
> the sword. Fetch the dog.
> Where is the pitch?—Here—
> Take hold of the torch
> and incense. Quick,
> open all doors.
> All of you watch.
> Put out the torch
> just as it is. Give
> silence while I
> strive for these women.
> Divine Lady, receive
> this food, these offerings.
>
> *Select Papyri* (Loeb) 3, No. 73.

There is one attendant, and several spectators sitting and watching.

Horace had or pretended to have had a feud with a witch named Canidia, and the fifth and seventeenth epodes are directed against her. In one of his *Satires* he puts into the mouth of the fertility god Priapus a vivid picture of the witches at work.

> With my own eyes I have seen Canidia come, her black dress
> tucked up, her feet bare, her hair loose,
> with Sagana, her senior, wailing, their sallow complexions
> terrifying to look at. They scratched up the soil
> with their nails, and tore a black lamb with their teeth
> to begin with. The blood drained into the trench, from which
> they purposed to draw the shades of the oracular dead.
> There was an effigy of wool, a second of wax, the woollen
> the larger, to hold the smaller in durance as punishment,
> the waxen standing in supplication, as if doomed
> to a slave's death. One witch invoked Hecate, the other
> cruel Tisiphone. You could see snakes and hounds
> of hell roaming round, and the moon blushing
> and hiding behind the tombs to avoid witnessing these acts.
> If I'm not telling the truth, may my head be messed with crows'
> white dung, and Julius, and that delicate sissy Pediatius,
> and Voranus the pickpocket come and piss and shit on me.
> No need to go into details of how the shades
> conversed with Sagana in shrill mournful echoes,
> and how they furtively buried in the soil the wolf's beard
> and a spotted snake's tooth, and how the fire blazed
> higher with the wax image and how I shuddered as I witnessed
> the words and actions of the two Furies—and took my revenge.
> I farted with the noise of a burst balloon
> and split my figwood arse. They took to their heels.
> Canidia's teeth and Sagana's high wig
> fell off and their herbs and enchanted
> love-knots. Laugh? You should have seen it!
>
> Horace *Satires* 1, 8, 23-50.

Some of this is literary and secondhand. But it is authentic black magic. Black for the powers of darkness; the sacrificial victim with its blood draining down to the underworld, the absence of fastenings on clothes, hair or shoes, which might fasten the magic on to themselves. The two images—the woollen one representing Canidia, the wax one of her lover—are a common form of magic all over the world.

We note too the wailing unearthly sounds and the use of the more savage wild animals.

There are many accounts of witchcraft in literature, none more gruesome than Lucan's account of a Thessalian witch named Erichtho raising the dead (6, 507-830).

One or two inscriptions from magical amulets will show the sort of formulations to be expected there.

Throttler-tearer-of-giants.
C. Bonner *Studies in Magical Amulets* p 169.

The spirit invoked has this immense power.

Iao sabaoth abrasax he-that-is be present.
ibid p 172.

Iao and abrasax are magical names. Iao is sometimes as here identified with the God of the Jews.

Bait is one, Athor one, their power one, Akori one.
Greetings, father of the world, greetings, triform god.
ibid p 175.

This is Egyptian-Greek. Bait is Horus, Athor Hathor, Akori the snake-goddess Buto; but the trinitarian formula suggests Christian Gnostic influence.

Lord of land and sea, you who shake the inhabited world, Ortineus of the nine forms, encompassed in clouds, marking out the aether, abolish all disease and foul designs of any man.
ibid p 183.

The style is hieratic. Ortineus is not known.

Hear me, you who have a home in Leontopolis, you who dwell in the sacred precincts, you who lighten and thunder, lord of mist and wind, you who own the heavenly necessity of eternal nature.

You are a god who acts swiftly, who hears prayer, who is of great glory, lion in form. Your name is Mios, Miosi, Harmios, Cusirmios, Phre, Simiephe, Phnonto, Light, Fire, Flame. Grant Ammonius your grace.
ibid p 184.

Ablanathanalba

ibid p 202.

A common magical palindrome. One of a large number of mystical and otherwise meaningless combinations of letters.

Curses, written on leaden tablets and buried in the ground, throw important light on popular religious belief. Here are two, one from the temple of Demeter in Cnidos, written in Greek, and the other from Hadrumetum in Africa, in Latin.

I consign to damnation, in the name of Artemis, Demeter, Kore and all the gods with Demeter, the person who at my demand does not return to me the cloaks, clothes and tunic which I left behind. Let him pay the penalty before Demeter, and if anyone else has any possessions of mine, let him be in torment till he confesses. And grant me purity and freedom, fellowship in drink, and food and house. I have been wronged, Lady Demeter.

W. Dittenberger *Sylloge*[3] 1179.

I invoke you, Spirit, whoever you are, and lay it upon you from this hour, this day, this moment that you torment and destroy the horses of the Green and White, kill and crush the charioteers Clarus Felix, Primulus, Romanus, leave no breath in their bodies. I lay it upon you in the name of one who set you free in season, the god of sea and air IAO IASDAO OORIO . . . AEIA

H. Dessau *Inscriptiones Latinae Selectae* 8753.

This last, no doubt from a betting man, is written in illiterate Latin, and accompanied by a drawing of the Spirit with a human head and cock's comb above it, a lamp in hand, standing in a boat, magic symbols, and the names of the horses. The last letters above are in Greek: to write in a foreign lettering intensified the magic: through the meaningless letters we can discern a shadow of the Jewish God, and a belief in the efficacy of vowels.

Tacitus tells a story in which the lead curse is combined with magic of other kinds.

Piso then returned to Seleuceia, to keep an eye on Germanicus' recurrent illness. It was a bad attack, worsened by his conviction that Piso had put a spell on him. Under the floor and inside the walls were found the disinterred remains of human bodies, magic formulas, curses, Germanicus' name scratched on lead tablets, human ashes charred and soaked in blood, and other magical devices designed to devote souls to the powers below.

Tacitus *Annals* 2, 69.

Remains of dead bodies would naturally provide efficacious death-magic. The other malignant objects may have been wild fig trees uprooted from tombs, cypress boughs, eggs or feathers of a screech-owl smeared with toad's blood, herbs from the witches' land of Thessaly, bones snatched from a hungry dog, actual or simulated waters from Lake Avernus.

All magic was of course not baleful and baneful. Apuleius, the second-century African author of *The Golden Ass*, who could tell a good witch-story when he chose, seems to have dabbled in magic himself, and was in fact put on trial for gaining a rich wife that way. He had no difficulty in laughing off the detailed charges (much as Pliny tells an excellent story of a farmer accused of securing a large yield by sorcery, who won acquittal by producing his tools in court). But in the course of his defence he does offer a cautious defence of magic before returning to the offensive.

You who so lightly bring charges against magic, do you realize that it is a scientific procedure blessed by the immortal gods, thoroughly cognizant with worship and adoration, religious of course, with an intimate knowledge of the divine, priestess of the powers of heaven, honoured from the time of its initiatiors, Zoroaster and Oromasdes? In Persia it is a cardinal part of the education of a king, and they do not lightly allow anyone to become a magician, any more than a king. Plato in another passage about a man named Zalmoxis, of Thracian nationality, but a practitioner of the same science, has left us the saying "Spells are beautiful words." In that case why shouldn't I be familiar with Zalmoxis' "fine words" or Zoroaster's priestly practices?

But if the gentlemen of the prosecution hold the popular view that a magician is a man in communication with the immortal gods who consequently acquires the power to do anything he wishes by spells of incredible efficacy, then I'm amazed that they are not scared to bring charges against one who on their own admission has such powers. It is impossible to find any protection against this mysterious divine power. Against other things you can. A man who brings a charge of murder comes into court with a posse of friends. A man who exposes a poisoner takes care what he eats. A man who denounces a burglar looks after his own property. But, if a man brings a capital charge against a magician, endowed with the powers they attribute to him, what friends, what precautions, what protection can save him from unseen, inescapable disaster? None. The man who believes in magic should be the last person to bring such a charge.

Apuleius Apology 26.

Zoroaster was the founder and prophet of the religion of Persia, but Oromasdes is no prophet but the god of light, Ahura Mazda. The Plato reference is *Charmides* 157A.

Lucian has a remarkable account of the religiosity prevalent in Asia Minor in the second century A.D. One of his most entertaining works is an exposure of a rogue and charlatan named Alexander of Abonuteichos.

Alexander made this dramatic entrance into his homeland after a long period. He was a striking figure, putting on an occasional show of madness and foaming at the mouth. This came easily to him by chewing soapwort, a plant used in dyeing, but others thought the foam an awesome visitation. He and his partner had a long time ago made in full detail a snake's head of linen, somewhat anthropomorphic in appearance, painted and very lifelike, which would open and close its mouth by the use of horsehair, and had a forked black tongue like a snake's darting out, also moved by hairs. They kept the snake from Pella ready, bringing it up at home, ready at the right moment to take its place on the stage with them in the leading role.

It was now time to make a start. Alexander put his plan into action. He went at dead of night to the excavations of the temple foundations—there was a pool of water, either rainwater or accumulated from somewhere or other. He had a goose's egg which he had already blown, containing a newly born snake. This he buried deep in the mud and slipped away again. At daybreak he leaped out into the city-centre, naked except for a gilded loincloth, brandishing his great scimitar, and tossing his loose hair like the devotees of the Great Mother in ecstasy. He mounted a high altar and made a speech, congratulating the people on their immediate prospect of receiving an epiphany of the god. Virtually the whole city, including women and children and senior citizens, had flocked together. They were awestruck, and went down on their knees in prayer. He made such unintelligible sounds, which might have been Hebrew or Phoenician, to impress an audience which had no notion what he was saying except that he kept bringing in the names of Apollo and Asclepius. Then he ran at the double to the temple-site, went straight to the excavations and the foundations of the oracle which he had previously prepared, waded into the water singing hymns to Asclepius and Apollo and in a loud voice began to invoke the god to come in blessing to the city. He called for a libation-bowl. One was given him, and he slipped it neatly into the pool and drew up water and mud—and the egg in which he had encased the god, sealing the edges of the piece stopping up the hole with pale wax and white lead. He took this in his hand and said "Here I have Asclepius." They already regarded the discovery of the egg in the water as a miracle, and could not take their eyes off him in their desire to see what was going to happen next. He cracked the egg and received the baby snake in the palm of his hand. When the watchers saw it wriggling and twining itself round his fingers, they raised a shout of welcome to the god and congratulations to the city. Each began to pile up the prayers greedily, praying the god for treasure, riches, health and every other blessing. Alexander went quickly back home with the newly born Asclepius, "twice-born where other men are once-born," mothered not by Coronis (good god, no!) or even by a crow, but by a goose. The whole population followed, everyone of them fired with religion and ecstatic with hope.

For some days he stayed at home, rightly anticipating that the story of what happened would bring large numbers of Paphlagonians together in a short time. When the city was overcrowded with people who lacked all brains and sense and were not in the least like human beings (those creatures who live on bread), but were indistinguishable from beasts of the field apart from outward appearance, Alexander went into a particular room and sat on a sofa, robed just like a god, and took the Asclepius from Pella on his lap (a snake, as I have already said, of considerable size and beauty), coiling it round his neck and letting its long tail pour from his lap and trail in part along the ground. Its head was the only part he kept out of sight, under his armpit (the snake would put up with anything). He displayed the linen head next to his own beard as if it belonged to the visible snake.

I'd like you to imagine a small room, not very light, and not admitting much daylight, containing an excited rabble, impressed in advance and buoyed up with hope. Picture them coming in. It must have seemed a miracle—that great snake emerging from the tiny reptile within a few days, with a human face at that, and tame. There was an immediate rush for the door and before they could get a proper look they were pushed out by those still coming in behind: another door had been opened in the opposite wall as an exit. . . .

Gradually Bithynia, Galatia and Thrace began to flock in. Everyone was talking about it, probably saying that he'd actually seen the god born, and subsequently touched him, that he'd grown to a great size and had a face like a man's. Paintings followed, and statues and statuettes, worked in bronze or silver. The god had to have a name, and was called Glycon as a result of a verse-instruction from the god. Alexander declaimed the line, "I am Glycon, Zeus' grandson, the Light of the World."

The time came to carry out the object of the exercise, to make oracular predictions. . . . Alexander gave advance notice to all comers that the god would utter prophecies, naming a particular day. He gave instructions that everyone should write his request or question on a scroll, fasten it and seal it with wax or clay or something of the sort. Then he personally took charge of the scrolls and went into the inner sanctuary (the temple was by now up and the stage prepared) ready to use a beadle and hierophant to summon the petitioners in due order, listen to the voice of the god, and then hand back the scroll with the seal unbroken, and the response written under the petition. The god would give an explicit response to the particular subject of the petition.

To a man like you, as, if I may say so, to myself, the trick is obvious and we can see through it easily enough, but to those snotty country-bumpkins it was miraculous and quite incredible. Of course he knew numerous methods for unfastening the seals. He simply read all the questions, gave his own answers to them, rolled up the papyrus again, sealed it, and handed it back. The recipients were bowled over. Words like these were for ever on their lips, "How could he know the petition when I sealed it securely with a distinctive seal before handing it to him, if not from some omniscient god?". . . .

So Alexander made his oracular pronouncements shrewdly enough, reinforcing his ingenuity with probable deductions. His responses to questions were sometimes darkly ambiguous, sometimes completely unintelligible, as this was his interpretation of the oracular style. Sometimes he offered encouragement or discouragement, making a reasonable guess at the right advice. As I said originally, he had a working knowledge of pharmacology, and sometimes prescribed diet or medical treatment. He made a great point of his *cytmides*, a name he invented for an ointment put together out of bear's fat. Expectations, promotions and inheritances he invariably deferred adding, "All will come about when I choose and when my prophet Alexander intercedes for you with prayer."

The charge fixed for a single response was a drachma and two obols. Don't underestimate it, my friend, or imagine that his income was small. He raked in seventy or eighty thousand drachmas a year. In their avaricious ambition people would submit ten or fifteen petitions at a time. He did not keep it all for himself or put it in the bank. He had a large staff of assistants, subordinates, informants, writers of oracles, recorders of oracles, scribes, sealers and interpreters, and paid each a fair wage.

It reached the point where he was sending emissaries abroad, to spread publicity about the oracle among the tribes round about, and to circulate the idea that he foretold the future, discovered runaway slaves, exposed thieves and robbers, identified the position of buried treasure, healed the sick, and in some cases even raised the dead. Crowds began rushing in from all quarters. There were sacrifices and offerings. The offerings for the god's prophet and apostle doubled in view of the appearance of the following oracle:

> I command that you honour my servant the Interpreter;
> I care little for riches but much for my Interpreter.
> > Lucian *Alexander or the False Prophet* 12-24.

The astonishing thing about this episode is the reputation that the oracle attained. Even the emperor Marcus Aurelius consulted it. The snake can be seen on coins, and the oracle was actually still in being more than fifty years after Alexander's death.

We may close this chapter with the account of the superstitious man given by Theophrastus somewhere around 300 B.C., but fairly timeless.

Superstition is of course a kind of cowardice in face of the divine.

We might characterize the Superstitious Man in the following terms. He washes his hands and asperses himself with water from the Three Springs and puts a laurel-leaf from a temple-precinct in his mouth before going out for the day. If a cat runs across the road he refuses to budge till someone else has passed or he has thrown three pebbles across the road. If he sees a snake in his house, he invokes Sabazios if it is red; if a sacred snake he establishes a shrine on the spot. On passing one of the smooth stones which stand at cross-roads, he pours a libation of oil from his flask and drops to his knees in worship before proceeding. If a mouse gnaws through a bag of barley, he goes straight off to the diviner to ask what he should do: if the answer is "Take it to the saddler's and have it patched" he ignores the advice, and goes through an apotropaic ritual. He's noted for continually purifying his house on the ground that it's been "visited" by Hecate. Owls hooting while he's out and about put him out of face: he won't go on without calling out "Athene is queen." He avoids treading on a grave or coming into contact with a dead body or a woman in childbirth: "better not risk pollution" he says. On the fourth and seventh of each month he has wine mulled for the whole family, goes out and buys myrtle-boughs, frankincense and holy pictures, and on his return spends the whole day offering sacrifices and garlands to the Hermaphrodites. If ever he has a dream he's off to the interpreters, the seers, the augurs, to ask what god or goddess he should propitiate. He applies for initiation into the Mysteries of Orpheus and pays a monthly visit to the hierophants accompanied by his wife, or, if she is not available, by his children and their nurse. He is meticulous about going down to the sea to asperse himself. If he sees a figure of Hecate at a crossroads with a crown of garlic, he goes straight back home, washes his head, and calls in priestesses telling them to purify him by carrying round a squill or young dog. If he sees a lunatic or an epileptic he shudders and spits into his lap.

Theophrastus *Characters* 16.

7. Beliefs About Death

In the Homeric poems the world of the dead is an empty, lifeless, hopeless world. The ghosts have no substance. Odysseus, alive in the world of the dead, talks with his mother.

> She finished speaking. I was sunk in thought, longing
> to clasp the spirit of my dead mother.
> Three times I moved swiftly forward, eager to clasp her;
> three times, like a shadow or a dream, she flitted
> out of my hands. Sharp anguish rose in my heart
> and I addressed her in winged words:
> "Mother, why do you not stay when I yearn to embrace you,
> that even in death we may join hands in love
> and both find comfort in shedding chill tears?
> Has Persephone in her majesty sent me no more than
> a phantom, to redouble my grief?"
> I finished speaking, and my dear mother promptly replied:
> "My son, ill-fated above all mortal men,
> Zeus' daughter Persephone is not guilty of deception;
> this is the way for mortals when anyone dies.
> The sinews no longer hold flesh and bones together.
> The strong power of blazing fire overwhelms
> them, as soon as the life leaves the white bones,
> and the spirit flutters and hovers like a dream."
>
> Homer *Odyssey* 11, 204-22.

So Achilles makes his famous declaration:

"Do not speak lightly of death to me, great Odysseus.
I should wish to be attached to the soil as the serf of another,
of some landless man with meagre resources,
rather than be lord of all the dead."

ibid 11, 488-9.

This mood was familiar in fifth-century Athens, and Euripides makes play with it in words which he puts, at the end of his life, into the mouth of his Iphigeneia.

Daylight is the loveliest thing for men to look upon.
What is below is nothingness. It is madness to pray
for death. Better a life of wretchedness than a glorious death.

Euripides *Iphigeneia at Aulis* 1250-2.

The Greek concept of Hades is closely parallel to the Hebrew Sheol.

What profit is there in my blood, in my descent to Sheol?
Can the dust acknowledge you or proclaim your truth?

Psalms 30:9.

A privileged few might be exempt from death, translated to the Isles of the Blest.

For them the sun shines strong below through our human night.
The ground before their city among lawns red with roses
shaded with incense-trees, heavy with golden fruit.
Some enjoy horses or wrestling, draughts
or music. Perfect bliss flowers among them.
It is a desirable country, full of fragrance.
As they are for ever placing incense of all kinds on the bright fire
       of the gods' altars.
Further away torpid streams of black darkness
belch out endless shadows.

Pindar *Dirges* fragment 95.

In Greece the Homeric picture was deeply ingrained. There are few more revealing passages in Greek literature than an exchange between Socrates and Glaucon in the last book of *The Republic:*

> "Have you never realized," I asked, "that our soul is immortal and never dies?" He stared at me in astonishment and said, "Good God, no! Are *you* capable of maintaining that?"
>
> Plato *Republic* 10, 608D.

In fact Plato more than any other brought the idea of immortality into intellectual circles. He produces a variety of arguments, one from the doctrine of Recollection, that all knowledge is recollection of what the soul has perceived before birth, another (in *The Republic*) claiming that any entity is destroyed by its peculiar evil, and that disease destroys the body only, but immorality (the soul's peculiar evil) does not destroy the soul (since bad men continue to live), and the soul is therefore immortal. The following passage from *Phaedo* is typical of his presentation:

> "Now," he said, "may we posit two forms of existence, visible and invisible?" "Right." "And the invisible is always the same, and the visible always changing?" "Yes." "Now we are made up of body and soul." "That is so." "Which class of existence would you say the body was more akin to?" "The visible, obviously." "And the soul? Is it visible or invisible?" "Invisible to human beings at any rate, Socrates!" "Well we use the words visible and invisible in terms of human sight, don't we?" "Yes." "Then what about the soul? Can it be seen or not?" "No." "Then it is invisible?" "Yes." "So the soul is more akin to the invisible than the body is, the body more akin to the visible than the soul." "That is a firm conclusion, Socrates."
>
> "Now we've been saying for some time that when the soul makes use of the body to answer a question, whether through seeing, hearing or one of the other senses (in this context the body means the senses), the body drags it into an area which is always changing, and it staggers dizzily around like a drunkard when it comes into contact with things like that." "Yes." "But when it carries on an investigation on its own, it launches into an area of purity, eternity, immortality, and changelessness. It is akin to these, and when it is allowed to operate on its own, it stays with no inclination to wander round, being eternally unchanging inasmuch as it is in contact with the eternally unchanging. This experience is

what we mean by wisdom." "Splendid, Socrates." "Now, from all we have said, now and earlier, which class of existence is the soul more akin to?" "After that exposition, Socrates, even a blithering idiot would agree that the soul is in every way more akin to the eternally changeless." "And the body?" "To the other class."

"Consider it this way. Soul and body are parts of the same individual. It's only natural for one part to be subordinate and the other to be master. Following this line of argument, which part savours more of divinity and which of mortality, do you suppose? I imagine you would agree that divinity is naturally equipped to command and mortality to be subservient." "Yes." "Then which does the soul resemble?" "Socrates, it is quite obvious that the soul is linked with divinity, the body with mortality." "Well, now, Cebes, bring your mind to bear on this! Does it follow from all we have said that the soul is like that form of existence which is divine, immortal, perceived by the mind, uniform, indissoluble and eternally changeless and the body like that form of existence which is human, mortal, multiform, perceived by the senses, dissoluble, and always changing? Is there anything to contradict this, my dear Cebes?" "No." "Well, in that case won't we expect the body to be subject to rapid dissolution and the soul to be completely or virtually indestructible?" "Surely."

Plato *Phaedo* 79A-80B.

In Rome the broadly Platonic view is found in Cicero's famous "Scipio's Dream."

He spoke, and I commented, "Africanus, if there is really a road to heaven open to those who have served their country well, then, even though ever since I was a boy I have followed in my father's footsteps and your own, and tried not to betray your high repute, from this moment I shall make even greater efforts in the prospect of such a great reward."

He replied, "Make these efforts in the realization that it is your body which is subject to death, not you. You are not the being depicted by your outward appearance. A man is his mind, not the material shape at which a finger can point. The real you is a god, you know, if activity, sentience, memory, foresight, and sovereignty over, control of, and power to move the body such as the supreme God exercises over the universe, are the marks of a god. The eternal God moves the universe which is in part subject to death. In the same way an immortal spirit moves the body, which is subject to dissolution.

"That which is forever in motion is eternal. That which receives from outside the motion which it passes on to something else is bound to end its life with its motion. Only that which is self-moved experiences unending motion because it never abandons itself; rather it is the origin and first cause of movement in all else that is subject to movement. A first cause has no beginning; everything stems from it, whereas it cannot stem from anything else, for if it has its birth from another source it would cease to be a first cause. As it has no beginning, so it has no end either. If the first cause were annihilated it could not be brought back into birth from some other source or produce anything else out of itself, granted the necessity of everything originating in a first cause. It follows that the first cause of motion is in something self-moved; this cannot come into being or pass away—or the whole universe would of necessity collapse and all nature grind to a halt lacking any power to provide the initial impulse to motion."

"In the light of this demonstration that the self-moved is eternal, it is impossible not to attribute this quality to souls. Things which receive their impulse to motion from outside are themselves inanimate. To be animate is to be moved by an inner impulse of one's own, the peculiar property of a living spirit. As spirit alone in the universe has the power of self-movement, it clearly has no beginning: it is eternal. Employ it in the highest tasks. The highest responsibilities relate to the advancement of your own country. A spirit dedicated to those responsibilities will soar on swifter wings to this its true homeland—even more rapidly if it peers out from the prison-house of the body, contemplates what lies beyond, and withdraws as far as possible from the body. For the spirits of those who have surrendered themselves to be slaves to the pleasures of the flesh and are driven by the lusts which minister to those to break the laws of god and man—these on leaving their bodies flit about the earth and do not return to this place until they have suffered many centuries of torment."

He left me. I awoke—and it was a dream.

Cicero *Republic* 6, 24, 26, 29.

This is the climactic final passage of Cicero's treatise on the state. The arguments are mostly taken from Plato *Phaedrus* 245C-E. Whether in Greek or Latin a translator is faced with an insoluble dilemma over the use of the words soul, spirit, mind and life, and the ambiguities should be remembered. In the last section it is interesting to see the uneasy alliance between the patriotic Roman statesman and the philosophical Greek mystic.

Some epitaphs assert immortality, but none of them is before the fourth century B.C., that is the time of Plato, and the majority, whether in Greek or Latin, are from the Roman period. An attractive example in Greek is the hexameter line from Alexandria:

I am undying, not mortal. —Marvellous. Who are you?—Isidora.
W. Peek "Griechische Epigramme aus Aegypten"
Bull. Soc. Arch. Alex. 27 (1932) 53.

In Latin we may quote such simple formulas as *aeternae animae* ("to the eternal soul"), found in Rome (*CIL* 6, 9240) or *vivis in eternum* ("you are alive for ever"), found in Madauros (F. Bücheler *Carmina Epigraphica Latina* 2270).

According to one strain of thought the universe is spherical and outside it is the stuff of divinity. This seeps through into the upper air (or aether) which is divine; this is why Socrates in Aristophanes' play *The Clouds* is lowered from above where he has been "treading the air and letting my thought move round the sun." When the principle of life (*psyche* or soul), which may on one side be identified with the mind or power of thought, but may also be identified with the breath (Latin *spiritus*; compare our "spirit") is dissociated from the body it is often envisaged as moving upwards to the divine *aether*, and sometimes as being translated into stars. An incidental remark by a character in Aristophanes is the best testimony to this.

Then it isn't true what they say, that when
we die, we become stars in the air.
Aristophanes *Peace* 832-3.

It is this fancy which Plato is playing with in a famous epigram on the death of Aster or Star.

Star, once you shone among the living as the Day Star,
now in death you shine as Evening Star among the dead.

> Plato in *Greek Anthology* 7, 670.

A Latin epitaph from Cologne shows a similar pattern of thought.

Timavius, loved name, hear our loving prayer.
The holy spirit within you escapes from the body
the body remains as earth, the spirit seeks the sky,
the spirit moves all things, the spirit is as God.
So you prophesied to me in comfort with your last breath.
So at your bidding I plucked flowers in thanks to the goddess of
    sorrow.

> F. Bücheler *Carmina Epigraphica Latina* 21526.

The central lines are clear enough. The meaning of the last line is not at all clear. I take it to mean that Timavius declared that his death should be an occasion for giving thanks to Proserpina, not for mourning.

The same sort of formulation continues in Christian epitaphs, as in this from the island of Ceos, long after the empire was firmly Christian.

Zosimianus, child of God, your sorrowing wife laid to rest
your outer covering here, in the lap of Mother Earth,
singing a hymn of mourning from lips of tenderness.
But your soul rose directly to heaven,
glad to proclaim your love to God your Father,
the love you bore for all, and all bore you.

> G. Kaibel *Epigrammata Graeca* 422.

The Stoics, inheriting some part of Plato's faith, were ambiguous about the fate of the soul. Seneca will serve as an example. In a fairly early work, perhaps about A.D. 40, he writes to Marcia, a friend of the empress Livia, to console her on the death of her son:

So there is no call for you to be dashing to your son's grave. What lies there is his inferior portion, a part that caused him much trouble, bones and ashes, no more a part of his real self than his clothes and other bodily coverings. He is complete, wholly departed, gone, leaving nothing of his real self behind on earth. He stayed for a little while over our heads while he was experiencing purification and shedding the imperfection which still adhered to him, and all the taint of our mortal life, then he soared to the heights and moved quickly to join the souls of the blessed. The company of the saints greeted him, the Scipios and Catos and those who would not cling to life but found freedom in poison, including your father, Marcia. There is one single family in heaven; still, he keeps his grandson close by him as he takes pleasure in the newness of light, teaches him the movements of the nearby stars, and is happy from his own wide experience, involving the element of conjecture, to instruct him in the mysteries of nature. Just as a stranger in a city he does not know is grateful for a guide, so your son in asking questions about the basic reality of heavenly things is grateful for a member of his family to give him explanations. He is instructed to direct his gaze on the earth far below him, and rather enjoys looking from a height on all that he has left behind. And you, Marcia, must live as in the sight of your father and son, but not as you knew them—far more exalted and stationed in the heavens. Blush at any worldly, common thought; blush to mourn your loved ones who have been translated to glory. They are allowed to move through the immense freedom of eternity. No seas interpose to block their path, no towering ranges, no tractless valleys, no shallows with shifting quick sand. There every course is level, movement easy and speedy; the very stars pass into their being and mingle with it.

                          Seneca *To Marcia on Consolation* 25.

To the Stoics the soul is formed of the divine fire, and therefore of the same substance as the stars.

But Seneca goes on to put into the mouth of Marcia's father a vision of a more ultimate destiny:

"When the time comes when the world will disappear in order to experience renewal, the whole physical world will be destroyed by its own forces, stars will rush upon one another, all the matter of the universe will take fire, and all that now glows with its own individual light will blaze up in a single conflagration. Then, when

God has taken the decision to reconstruct the universe, and the world is collapsing, we too, blessed souls who have been granted eternal life, shall form a small addition to that colossal devastation and shall be turned back into our original elements."

Blessed is your son, Marcia, who has already found that out!
ibid. 26, 6-7.

One wonders whether the Stoics really found consolation in the thought of our being resolved into our original elements. There is a similar account in the 102nd *Letter* in which he describes his "pleasure in investigating—or rather believing—the immortality of the soul."

One explanation of ghosts is that they are souls separated from the body but anchored down by impurity and unable to rise. So Plato:

You must recognize that the corporeal involves weight, heaviness, earthly ties, visibility. A soul which retains an element of the corporeal is weighed down, dragged back to the visible world, out of fear of the invisible world of Death, and so, in the popular belief, it flits round tombs and cemeteries, where shadowy appearances of souls have been actually seen, apparitions produced by souls which have not been completely liberated but retain an element of the visible, which accounts for their appearance to the eye.

Plato *Phaedo* 81 C-D.

One idea is that the dead man continues a life of a sort within the tomb.

This is my eternal home.
Here is rest from labour.
F. Bücheler *Carmina Epigraphica Latina* 225, 1-2.

So the wealthy may have their tombs built in the form of houses, or endow an annual dinner at the tomb, in which the dead man would share. The child's toys and women's ornaments buried in the tomb may not, as is often said, be for use in "the other world," but in the tomb itself. The strewing of flowers on a grave was in origin the offering of life-power to the dead, and red flowers, which were generally used, were a blood-surrogate, but as time went on this thought tended to be lost, and some tombstones express joy in the thought that life still flows from the dead into flowers planted on or near the tomb.

> Pomptilla, may your bones blossom into violets and lilies,
>   may you flower in rose-petals,
> sweet-scented crocus and ageless amaranth,
>   and blossom in a lovely white bloom
> to rival the narcissus and much-mourned hyacinth,
>   that generations to come may have a flower from you.
>   G. Kaibel *Epigrammata Graeca* 547a, 1-6.

Similar in concept is the often abbreviated STTL *sit terra tibi levis* "may the earth lie lightly on you."

The very common formula in Latin "Eternal sleep" or, as it appears frequently in Gaul and Germany, "The Divine Dead and eternal rest," is not, I think, nihilistic, though human beings have an immense capacity for holding irreconcilable ideas in combination. Rather the dead are alive but at rest. They may awaken for the annual celebration; it is hoped that they will not awaken at other times.

Of the Hellenistic philosophies Epicureanism was unique in proclaiming death as the end. This is clearly put by Epicurus in the letter to Menoeceus:

> Grow familiar with the idea that death is nothing to us. Good and evil depend entirely on sensation. Death is the elimination of sensation. So the true knowledge that death is nothing to us makes mortality enjoyable, not by adding to it an eternity of time, but by removing the desire for immortality. When a man has just comprehended that there is nothing to be feared in the absence of life, he finds nothing to be feared in life, itself. It is stupid for a man to say that he is afraid of death not because it will be painful when it comes but because it is painful in prospect. When anything is not grievous in actuality, any part caused by anticipation of it is

illusory. So death, the most spine-chilling of all ills, is nothing to us, since so long as we exist death is not present, and once death is present we no longer exist. Death is nothing to the living, for whom it does not exist, or for the dead, who no longer exist themselves.

Epicurus in Diogenes Laertius 10, 124-5.

This finds magnificent expression in Latin in the third book of Lucretius. He produces some thirty (they are differently counted by different scholars) arguments for the mortality of the soul and then comes to a passage of triumphant eloquence:

> So death is nothing to us, it does not matter one iota,
> since the nature of the mind is established as mortal!
> Just as in the past we felt no distress,
> when the Carthaginians came to conflict from every side
> and the whole world was shaken by the turmoil of war,
> shivered and shook under high heaven,
> and no-one could tell to whose dominion would fall
> all human power by land and sea,
> so, when we no longer exist, when body and soul
> are severed from each other,
> from whose union we are created,
> nothing at all can happen to us, or affect
> our senses, seeing that we no longer exist,
> even though earth and sea, or sea and sky are tossed together.
> Even if the nature of our mind and soul did allow us
> to feel, after they were separated from the body,
> that still would not affect us, for we are formed
> from the conjunction and coordination of body and soul.
> Even if time were to bring together our matter
> after death, and restore it to its present constitution,
> and the light of life were granted us again,
> even that event would not affect us,
> when the thread of our consciousness was once snapped.
> We may have existed before, but it does not affect us
> now, or no pain from those beings to be affects us.
> When you look back on the immeasurable extent
> of all past time, and the variety of motions
> experienced by matter, you could readily believe
> that these same atoms, of which we now consist,
> existed in the same arrangement often in time past,

and yet we cannot recapture the fact in memory,
because there is a gap of life in between, and all
the motion has widely dispersed from those sensations.
If anyone is to experience pain and sorrow in the future,
the man who is to have the unfortunate experience must exist
at that time. Death eliminates this, and prevents the existence
of the man for whom these disasters would accumulate
so we can be sure that there is nothing to fear in death,
that the man who does not exist cannot be wretched, and
      that it does not
matter a bit whether he ever existed in the past,
once deathless death has ended a life subject to death.

Lucretius 3, 830-69.

Some epitaphs show a belief in annihilation after death which may be affected by the spread of Epicurean ideas. One of the most famous is found in several variants, both in Greek and Latin, mainly in Rome and Italy, but also in Gaul and Africa. It is so familiar that it is even found abbreviated NFFNSNC (*CIL* 5,2893 cf 1813). This is *non fui fui non sum non curo*.

I was not.   I was.   I am not.   I care not.

It is likely that this formula was in fact Epicurean in origin. So too, in view of the Epicurean polemic against traditional mythology, may this be:

Traveller, do not pass by my epitaph.
Stand and listen, and go away a wiser man.
There is no boat in Hades, no ferryman Charon,
no janitor Aeacus, no watchdog Cerberus.
All of us beneath the ground in death
have become bones and ashes; there is nothing beside.
I have told you the truth. On your way, traveller,
or you will think that even in death I talk too much.

G. Kaibel *Epigrammata Graeca* 646.

Sometimes this view is combined with a kind of popular Epicureanism, which is in fact a misunderstanding of Epicurus: "Eat, drink and be merry, for tomorrow we die." This is given an unexpected twist in the so-called epitaph of Sardanapallus, a literary conceit, which is however echoed in numerous tombstones.

> Realize your mortality and lift up your heart
> and enjoy yourself. There's nothing to hope for after death.
> I once ruled mighty Nineveh, and now I am dust.
> All that I have is what I ate, my revels and the delights
> of love. All my glorious possessions are left behind.
> This is wise advice about life for mankind.
>
> Anon in Greek Anthology
Planudean Appendix 27.

It is a thought which finds marvellous expression in the once Epicurean Horace:

> The snows have disappeared; the grass is returning to the fields,
>   the leaves to the trees;
> the earth is changing; the rivers sink
>   as they pass their banks;
> the Grace with the nymphs and her two sisters takes courage
>   to dance naked.
> "Do not hope for immortality," proclaim the year and the hour
>   which speeds on the kindly day.
> The cold melts before the west wind, summer tramples on spring,
>   doomed herself when once
> fruitful autumn has harvested her bounty, and now
>   black winter is back.
> Still, the moons in the sky are swift to make up their losses.
>   *We* have but to go down
> with good Aeneas, wealthy Tullus, and Ancus,
>   we are dust and shadow.
> Who knows if the gods above will add
>   tomorrow to today?
> All that you give to yourself will evade the grasping
>   clutch of your heirs.
> Once you are dead, and Minos has pronounced his solemn
>   judgement on you,
> Torquatus, your family, your eloquence, even your religion
>   will not restore you.
> Diana could not free virginal Hippolytus
>   from the darkness of Hades;

> Theseus had no power to snap the chains of Death holding
> his beloved Pirithous.
>
> Horace *Odes* 4, 7.

Aeneas, the founder of Rome; Tullus and Ancus, legendary kings; Minos, judge of the dead; Hippolytus, son of Theseus and servant of Diana (Artemis); Pirithous, friend and ally of Theseus, who accompanied him in his assault on Hades but did not return. Horace puts the traditional mythology to good effect in a nihilistic poem.

The general absence of hope is seen in the failure of the Attic orators to console the family of the dead with the prospect of life beyond death. Another aspect of the same lack of hope is the precise record of age at death, even to months and days. The implication is that life on earth is the only real life and every day must be counted. It is natural that the same formula passes into Christian inscriptions:

> Gentianus faithful in peace, who lived twenty-one years eight months sixteen days. Intercede for us in your prayers, for we know that you are in Christ.
>
> O. Marucchi *Christian Epigraphy* 117.

But not always. Christian epitaphs can often be recognized by their indifference to the exact age at death; for Christians it was the life beyond which counted:

> To the Divine Dead. Flavius Antigonus Papias, a Greek, lived for more or less sixty years at which point he restored the soul the Fates had lent him. Septimia Domina set up this stone.
>
> *Roman Inscriptions of Britain* 955.

Even here the pagan formula "To the Divine Dead" and the idea of the fates remain.

But in general there was no doubt some vague and unformulated belief in survival. We can see it in the festivals of the dead. At Athens, for example, there was the Genesia when the whole citizen body honoured their ancestors; the Nemesia when the anger of the dead was appeased; and the Anthesteria, a spring festival when the dead swarmed back to life, and were eventually dismissed with the cry "Out of doors, Keres, Anthesteria is over." We have an important description of a parallel festival at Rome, the Lemuria, which took place on 9 May:

> When from the Nones the Evening Star has three times shown
>   his lovely face,
>   three times Pheobus routed the stars,
> there will be by night an ancient religious ritual, the Lemuria,
>   bringing gifts to the silent shades.
> The year was once shorter, they knew no religious expiations,
>   two-headed Janus did not lead the months.
> Even then they brought offerings to the ashes of the dead,
>   descendant honouring ancestor.
> The month was May, named from the Great Majority;
>   it keeps part of the tradition.
> When midnight comes, bending silence to sleep,
>   and dogs and birds are hushed,
> the man who honours traditional religion and fears the gods,
>   rises, no knots near his feet,
> and makes a sign, thumb between knuckles
>   to avert silent encounter with a ghost.
> He cleanses his hands with water from a spring,
>   turns, takes black beans,
> faces away, and throws them down saying "These are my
>   offerings;
>   with these beans I redeem me and mine,"
> Nine times he says it without looking back. It is thought that
>   the ghost
>   follows unseen and gathers them.
> Again he touches water and clangs Temesan bronze,
>   asking the shade to leave his house.
> Nine times he says "Spirits of my fathers, be gone,"
>   then looks back in the knowledge of ritual fulfilled.
>
>   Ovid *Fasti* 5, 419-44.

The year once began in March (December means the tenth month) so the *februa* or expiations appropriate to February were not known. Ovid derives May from *maiores*, ancestors. Knots might bind the householder. The clenched fist, with thumb thrust between the first two fingers is a well known apotropaic gesture called in Italy *la fica*, the fig. The number three is prominent. The beans, black for the dead, are surrogates for the family. Because of their shape they were phallic emblems, and they were associated with life. Bronze (pre-iron) is used for the apotropaic sound.

One of the commonest Latin formulations on tombstones is D M, *dis Manibus* ("to the Divine Dead"). There *is* ambiguity. The Manes are thought of as the spirits of the dead but also as spirits of death, who control the dead. But there is no doubt that the general sense is one of supernatural power continuing in association with the shades of the dead. Even the Lares, the familiar household gods of the Romans, have been thought to be originally ancestral spirits, buried in the ground and so blessing and fructifying the soul, and entering the home and blessing it.

The vague belief is sometimes mixed with the traditional mythology of the underworld, and combined with the thought of re-union after death. This is exquisitely used by Martial in a poem on the death of a little girl:

> Fronto my father, Flaccilla my mother, look after
>   this girl, my love, my darling,
> that poor little Erotion may not be frightened of the black shadows,
>   or of the monstrous jaws of the hound of hell.
> She would have passed the chills of only her sixth winter,
>   but she lived six days too few.
> I'd like her to play carefree, watched by protectors of your age,
>   to chatter, with my name on her lisping tongue.
> Don't let the turf lie hard on her tender bones—and earth,
>   don't be heavy on her; she was not so to you.
>   Martial 5, 34.

Even there the "faith" is blended with the thought of the body lying in the tomb. An actual epitaph shows a similar hope of re-union after death:

> In honour of the holy dead. Furia Spes makes this offering to my dear husband L. Sempronius Firmus. As I learned, we were a boy and girl linked alike in love. I lived with him for too short a time; at the time when we should have been living we were torn apart by a cruel hand. So I beseech you, Holy Power of the Dead, hold my beloved one in good care, and be kind enough to grant him in the

hours of night that I may see him, and persuade fate to let me come
to him swiftly and gently.

CIL 6, 18817.

These are moving in their tenderness. But the vague beliefs
must also have been often fearful. Particularly must this have been
true where Etruscan influence was strong. The Etruscan tombs
often show horrific portrayals of the demon-torturers of the underworld. The Epicureans who tried to allay fears of this kind were
not tilting at windmills:

> You can be certain that all that tradition records
> in the depths of Acheron, we experience in this life.
> There is no Tantalus in abject fear of a great rock
> menacing him, motionless with fruitless fear, as in the story.
> Rather in this life groundless fears of the gods assail
> mankind, and the fall they fear is the fall of chance events.
> No Tityos lies in Acheron with vultures gnawing his innards.
> Even in that great body there is not enough for them
> to find to peck at for all eternity.
> Extend his vast body as wide as you will,
> with limbs spread to cover not just nine
> acres, but the whole surface of the earth,
> still he will not be able to bear to the end an unending pain
> or provide food from his own body for ever.
> For us Tityos is here, sunk in love,
> torn up by things that fly away, consumed by anguished
>   anxieties,
> broken by love and all its lusts.

Lucretius 3, 978-94.

He goes on through Sisyphus and the Danaids and all the tortures of Tartarus, and rationalizes them, ending "The life of fools
becomes a hell on earth." It is a brilliant passage. But, although
Cicero calls the myths of Hades "old wives' tales," there must
have been old wives of all ages and both sexes to believe them. The
Epicureans were assailing actual fears.

Real faith in something after death belongs for the most part to
the Mystery Religions. To these we must finally turn.

8. The Mystery-Religions

A mystery is a closed secret revealed only to initiates. It is quite literally something you keep mum about. The mystery-religions of the Graeco-Roman world offered to their initiates the promise of blessedness after death through revelation and communion with the divine on conditions of ritual and moral purity. Some of the cults were of respectable antiquity, but their great age was the Hellenistic-Roman period.

The most famous of the mystery-religions was the cult of Demeter and Kore (Persephone, the Maid) at Eleusis.

The Homeric Hymn to Demeter evokes the legend with many aetiological touches; it is very long.

> I am beginning a hymn of the dread goddess, Demeter of the
>   lovely hair,
> and of her neat-ankled daughter, whom Aidoneus
> kidnapped and ravished, a gift from far-seeing thundery Zeus.
> Homer Hymn 2, 1-3.

> Sharp pain gripped her heart, and she tore
> with her hands the covering on her divine hair,
> let her dark cloak slip from her shoulders,
> sped like a bird, over land and sea
> in search. But no one would tell her
> the truth, no god, no human,
> no true message came from the birds.

For nine days our Lady Deo went to and fro
over the earth, with lighted torches in her hands.
In her grief she never touched ambrosia
or the rich drink of nectar, never washed her body.
But when the tenth dawn shone with its light upon her,
Hecate with a lamp in her hands met her
and told her the story.

ibid 40-53.

She comes to Eleusis.

Then Metaneira filled a cup with sweet wine
and gave it her, but she refused, saying she was not permitted
to drink red wine. She told them to mix barley meal
and water with smooth mint and give it her to drink.
The other mixed the Potion and gave it to the goddess as
            instructed.
Almighty Lady Deo received it for the sake of the sacrament.

ibid 206-11.

The sacramental Potion was part of the Mystery-ritual.

She reveals herself.

"I am Demeter, honoured by all, the greatest source
of benefit and happiness to gods and mortals alike.
Now all the people are to build me a great temple
with an altar by it, beneath the sheer wall of the city
on the rising ground above the Callichorus spring.
I will introduce my rites in person, and you in future
may perform them religiously and with my approval."

ibid 268-74.

But she puts a blight on the earth.

When they had finished and rested from their labours,
they all went home. But golden-haired Demeter
sat there, away from all the other blessed gods,
waiting, wasting in desire for her bosomy daughter.
She brought all over the fertile earth a year
of cruel devastation on mankind. No seed
sprang from the soil; rich-crowned Demeter kept it under.
The oxen drew the curved ploughs in the fields to no purpose;
the white barley fell upon the soil fruitlessly.

She would have destroyed the whole race of mankind
with bitter starvation, and deprived the gods of Olympus
of their cherished honours in gifts and sacrifices,
only Zeus realized and took it to heart.

ibid 301-13.

Persephone is released by Aidoneus, king of the dead.

"Go, Persephone, to your mother in her dark robes,
keep a kindly disposition towards me,
do not look so excessively depressed.
Among the immortal gods I am not an unworthy partner for you;
I am Father Zeus' own brother. While you are here,
you shall be queen of all that lives and moves,
you shall have the highest honours among the immortal gods.
Those who do not appease your power with sacrifice
in religious ceremony, offering due gifts,
shall face eternal punishment for their crimes."

ibid 360-9.

In a scene of joy the goddesses are reunited, and Demeter is
persuaded to relent.

She spoke, and rich-crowned Demeter listened,
and immediately sent the corn sprouting in the fertile fields,
till the whole wide earth was heavy with leaves
and flowers. She went to the kings who deliver justice,
Triptolemus, and Diocles the charioteer,
sturdy Eumolpus, and Celeus, leader of his people,
and showed them the conduct of her rites, and revealed her
          mysteries
to them all, Triptolemus, Polyxeinus, and Diocles as well,
solemn mysteries, which none may transgress or search into
or publish; for a healthy respect for the gods checks his voice.
Blessed among men on earth is he who has seen these things.
But he who is uninitiate in the holy rites, who has no lot in them,
does not enjoy a like fate when he lies in death beneath broad-
          spreading darkness.

ibid 470-82.

It has been argued that the promise of the last three lines is not so
much of life after death as of a different quality of life after death, but
the last line is somewhere near annihilation. The climax of the Mysteries was something seen, clearly (though it has been denied) a dra-

matic reenactment of the myth, culminating in a brilliant light, and
the display of a sacred ear of corn.

Plutarch, without of course revealing the secrets, gives an account of the process of initiation and revelation.

So we describe the soul which has passed beyond as one of the
holy dead because it is wholly changed and transformed. In this
world it lacks knowledge, except at the very moment of expiring;
at that point it has an experience similar to those who receive the
inspiration of initiation into the Great Mysteries. (There is a simi-
larity, verbal and actual, between expiration and inspiration.) First
comes aimless wandering, tiring movements in a circle, uncertain
explorations through darkness getting nowhere, then before the
actual fulfilment, terrors of every kind, shuddering, knees shak-
ing, sweat pouring down, a feeling of awe. Then suddenly a marvellous light comes to meet him and he enters open fields and a
land of purity; there are voices dancing and majestic and holy
things to greet the ear and eye. Now he has found fulfilment, he is
an initiate, and he walks freely among all this with a garland on his
head, celebrating and companying with saintly men. He looks
down on the great mass of those living on earth, uninitiated, un-
purified, packed together in mud and fog, trampling one another
underfoot, and out of fear of death clinging to their evils because
they do not believe in the blessings beyond. From this you can see
clearly that the soul's entanglement with the body and imprison-
ment in it are really contrary to nature.
　　　　　Plutarch *On the Soul* fragment in Stobaeus 4, 52, 49.

I have altered slightly but tried to convey reasonably the effect of the
word-play at the beginning. Despite the scepticism of G.E. Mylonas
(*Eleusis and the Eleusinian Mysteries* pp 264 ff) it is hard to believe that
this is not an account of initiation at Eleusis.

Cicero, who was an initiate, gives an account of what initiation
at Eleusis meant.

Atticus: I imagine you make an exception of those Mysteries in
which we were initiated ourselves.

Marcus: I will surely do so. Your Athens has plainly made many
outstanding contributions to human life, gifts from heaven, but

none better than those Mysteries. They educated us out of a life of barbarous rusticity into civilization. The ceremonies are called initiations, and we recognize in them the first principles of living. We have gained from them the way of living in happiness and dying with a better hope.

Cicero *Laws* 2, 14, 36.

Cicero, in discussion with his brother Quintus and his friend the Athenian Atticus, is discussing legislation against uncontrolled religions, but explicitly exempts the Eleusinian Mysteries.

So too in a Greek epigram of much the same period.

You were always a man of the armchair, never sailed the sea,
    never trod the main roads,
yet you made your way to Attica to watch the famous
    long nights of Demeter's mysteries,
which have lifted all burdens from your mind in life, and when
    you join
    the majority, made it lighter.

Crinagoras in *Greek Anthology* 11, 42.

Dionysus was another deity who had his Mysteries. We are aware of them in a number of different forms. One can be seen in the glorious wall-paintings in the Villa of the Mysteries on the edge of Pompeii. Here the central figures were Dionysus and his bride Ariadne, and the revelation is of the power of life contained in a phallus. The initiate, a woman, is born into the world of Dionysus, and passes through symbolic death into resurrection and union with the god.

One form of the Dionysiac Mysteries is associated with the legendary figure of Orpheus, a kind of double of Dionysus, a musician with the power to charm the forces of nature, and the rulers of the underworld. With his cult went a complex myth of the dying and rising god, and man with elements of divinity in a strong covering of grossness.

Orphic beliefs in a judgement after death are reflected in Pindar's second Olympian ode written for a Sicilian dictator's victory in the chariot-race in 476 B.C.

Wealth embellished with excellences brings different rewards
in due season, urging the mind to profound pursuits.
It is a cynosure, man's
true light. But if a man, possessing wealth, knows the future
that lawless spirits suffer immediate punishment
on earth after death, and that below the earth there is one
who sentences with ineluctable sternness sins committed
in this kingdom where Zeus rules,
but that with equal nights for ever
and equal days the sun shines on the good; they enjoy
a life of lightened labour, not troubling the earth with strong hands
or the sea's waters
for a fruitless livelihood, but living a life
without sorrow, if they joyed to keep their oaths, alongside
the gods they honoured (the others endure torment no eye can bear).
All who, dwelling in either world,
have had the strength three times to keep their life completely free
from wrongdoing, take Zeus' road to the tower of Cronos. There
the ocean-winds blow
round the Isles of the Blest, and flowers of gold flame out,
some from glorious trees on land, others growing in the water.
They twine fillets of these and garlands round their hands
according to the strict judgement of Rhadamanthys,
the ever-ready fellow-judge with the mighty Father,
husband of Rhea whose throne is high over all.

                                        Pindar *Olympians* 2, 53-77.

> This is an important passage. We see in it the movement of *arete* (ex-
> cellence) from social effectiveness in the more obvious senses (wealth
> or prowess) to virtue. We can see how the mystery-religions take up
> for example the traditional religious sanction against oath-breaking
> and use it as the basis for a wider morality. The passage contains the
> doctrine of reincarnation: three lives of righteousness suffice to
> escape from the sorrowful weary wheel (see below). Rhadamanthys
> is the mythological son of Zeus and Europe, and judge of the dead.

From Magna Graecia we have some gold tablets, perhaps
though not certainly of Orphic origin.

> You will find within the halls of Hades a spring on the left
> and close to it a white cypress standing.
> Do not go near this spring.
> You will find another, cool water pouring

from the Lake of Memory. Guards stand in front of it.
Say "I am a child of earth and starry heaven,
but my race is of heaven. You know this for yourselves.
I am parched with thirst and perishing. Quick, give me
cold water pouring from the Lake of Memory."
Then they will freely allow you to drink from the sacred spring,
and thereafter you will reign with the other demi-gods.

Gold plate from Petelia:
O. Kern *Orphicorum Fragmenta* 32a.

Queen of the dead, I come pure from a pure people,
and you, Eucles, Eubouleus and the other immortal gods.
For I claim to be of your blessed race,
but fate and other immortal gods overpowered me
. . . the flash of lightning.
I have flown out of the sorrowful, weary wheel,
I have come with speeding feet for the crown of my desire,
I bury my head in the lap of Our Lady, the Queen of the dead.
"Blessed and happy one, you shall be a god, a mortal no longer."
I am a kid fallen into milk.

Gold plate from Thurii: *ibid* 32c.

These gold plates date from the fourth or third century B.C. They
were found in graves, and give instructions to the soul of the dead.
The concept of a choice of direction in death as in life is an old one.
The Queen is Persephone. Eucles ("the fair-famed") is her consort
Pluto. Eubouleus ("excellent in counsel") appears in a hymn as their
son. It is sometimes a title of Zeus, but here is perhaps a title of Dionysus. The white cypress is a mystery: probably the tree of death is
magically transformed into a tree of light. "I am a kid fallen into milk"
is clearly an expression of rebirth. Dionysus was seemingly worshipped in the guise of a kid and it is the mystic's hope to be reborn
into the god's being. In the Villa of the Mysteries at Pompeii one of
the scenes shows a kid being suckled by a Panisca.

We also have a number of hymns from some unorthodox sect
of the Roman imperial period.

Persephone, mighty Zeus's daughter, blessed one, come,
goddess only-begotten, and receive our sacred offerings,
honoured bride of Pluto, kindly giver of life,
you who below the depths of the earth rule the gates of Hades,
dealer of justice, lovely in your hair, pure offspring of Deo,

mother of the Kindly Goddesses, Queen of the dead,
whom Zeus in secret union fathered as his daughter,
mother of Eubouleus of the many forms and loud noise,
playfellow of the Seasons, Light-bringer, splendid to look on,
noble, omnipotent Maiden, teeming with fruits,
glorious in brightness, horned, the sole desire of mortals,
goddess of spring, taking joy in the meadow-grass,
showing your sacred body in the flowers with their promise of fruit,
your bridal bed the rape of autumn harvest,
you alone are life and death for mankind in our distress,
Persephone—you produce and you destroy all things—
blessed goddess, hear! Grant us fruits from the earth;
flower with peace and kindly health
and a blessed life, which brings a rich old age
to your halls, my Lady, and to Pluto, mighty in goodness.

Orphic Hymn 30.

> The interaction here between the mystery-religion, the fertility of the
> land, and the promise of eternal life is clear. In the line beginning
> with the goddess's name there is a kind of pun. Persephoneia, or
> rather Phersephoneia, is derived from *pherein* ("produce") + *phoneu-*
> *ein* ("destroy").

A fragment from Euripides' lost play, *The Cretans*, throws a
little light on one version of the Mysteries of Dionysus. The chorus
is addressing Minos:

Son of Pheonician Europe
and almighty Zeus, ruler
of Crete and its hundred cities,
I am come, leaving the holy shrines
roofed with beams of local wood,
shaped with an axe of steel,
their cypress joists bound
firm with bull's hide glue.
We have led a life of holiness since
entering the Mysteries of Zeus of Ida.
In the thunder of night-travelling Zagreus
and the Feast of Raw Flesh I have found fulfilment.
I have brandished torches for the Mother of the Mountains.
I have been purified
and named Bacchus of the Curetes.

I wear clothes of white, and shun
mortal birth and will not touch
the burial of the dead and avoid
consuming living creatures.

Euripides fragment 475.

There is a discussion of this passage in A.B. Cook's monumental *Zeus*
I 648. Plainly there is some blurring at the edges. The Mysteries here
are those of Zeus, but the titles of Zagreus (which the Greeks translated "Great Hunter") and Bacchus are found of Dionysus also, and
the Feast of Raw Flesh is his. The initiates speak of three rituals—the
making of thunder, no doubt through drums, by which they become
identified with the God of Thunder; the Feast of Raw Flesh, a communion in which they consume the flesh of the god in his animal
form; and the rite of Torches, an aspect of the Sacred Marriage between the Sky-Father and Mountain-Mother. In addition their lives
must show ceremonial purity.

From Smyrna in the second century A.D., perhaps from the
sanctuary of Dionysus Briseus on the outskirts of the city we have
a remarkable inscription showing some of the prescriptions of the
Mysteries of Dionysus, set out in hexameters.

SET UP BY MENANDER'S SON . . . THE THEOPHANT

All you who enter the precinct and shrines of Bromios,
abstain for forty days after exposing
a young child, for fear of divine wrath:
the same number of days for a woman's miscarriage.
If death and doom overshadow one of your household,
keep away from the forecourt the third part of a month;
if pollution come from another's house
through a dead body, stay apart for three days.
Do not approach the altars of our Lord in black clothes.
Do not begin the sacred feast until the dishes have been blessed.
Do not serve an egg at the sacred meal in the mysteries of Bacchus.
Refrain from burning the heart on the holy altar.
Abstain from mint . . .
and the abominable root of beans . . .
Tell the initiates about the Titans . . .
It is not right to use reeds as castanets . . .
on the days on which initiates offer sacrifices. . .
or to carry. . . .

J. Keil *Inschriften aus Smyrna* p. 17.

Some of the inscription is lost, and the precise meaning of some
phrases controversial, but the general sense is clear. The respect for
children is a noteworthy part of the mysteries of Dionysus; we know
of a child initiate, who died aged 3 years and 2 months. The absence
of any prohibition of those who have had sexual intercourse is noteworthy: the Dionysiac mysteries were evidently, as we would say,
permissive. There are assimilations to the Orphics (the sacredness of
the Cosmic Egg; the myth of the wicked Titans) and Pythagoreans
(abstention from beans). The priest, whose name is lost, is called a
theophant: this suggests that the mysteries included an epiphany of
the god.

We pass next to the Mysteries of Cybele and Attis. Cybele is
one form of the Great Mother, who is found all over the Near East.
There were, so to speak, two levels of service of Cybele. Her
priests were eunuchs, self-castrated in ecstasy.

On set days the people crowd into the temple precincts and many
Galli, that is the holy men of whom I was speaking, perform the
ceremonies, cutting their arms and presenting their backs to one
another for lashing. Many of those present are playing flutes,
many are beating tambourines, some are singing sacred songs
under divine inspiration. This operation takes place outside the
temple, and those who are responsible for it do not enter the temple.

This is the time when men become Galli. While the others are
playing the flute and performing these rites, frenzy is already descending on many of them—and many who have come as spectators join in. I will tell you what they do. The young man for whom
this is destined throws off his clothes, rushes into the middle with
a loud cry and picks up a sword (I imagine that it has been lying
there for many years). He grasps it and instantly castrates himself.
Then he rushes through the city carrying his severed organ in his
hands. He throws it into any house he likes, and from that same
house takes feminine clothing and ornaments. This is the castra-
tion-ceremony.

When Galli die they are not buried in the same way as other
men. If a Gallus dies, his associates take up his body and carry it
outside the city. They set him down together with the bier on
which they carried him, cover them over by throwing stones
down on them, and having done this go back home. They observe
an interval of seven days before entering the temple; to enter be-

fore that would be an act of impiety. They observe the following regulations. If one of them sets eyes on a dead body, he does not enter the temple on that day, but enters it on the next day only after an act of purification. All of the dead man's relatives observe an interval of thirty days, and shave their heads before entering; to enter before doing this would be an act of impiety.

Lucian The Syrian Goddess 50-3.

> This is of course a sceptical account, but Lucian claims that it is made from first-hand observation. The myth of Cybele and Attis clearly has to do with fertility. Curiously, it is not clear whether the severing of the genitals was intended as an offering of the male fertility exclusively to the service of the goddess, or the severing of the channel of emission, so that the fertility (believed to reside in the head) remained with the priests, and in that way was at the goddess's service, while they were destined for immortality through not losing their life-power. The Roman Senate introduced the worship of Cybele during the Second Punic War, and were promptly horrified by what they had done, and banned the Romans from participation. A century and a half later Catullus wrote a marvellously imaginative poem on the theme.

From the second century A.D. we have records of rites designed for the ordinary worshipper, man or woman. The *taurobolium* or baptism in bull's blood, or the lesser rite the *criobolium* or baptism in ram's blood were the entry into eternal life. Sometimes it seems as if the rite is regarded as having absolute efficacy, sometimes it was renewed after twenty years. It might be undergone vicariously, or as a public ritual for public safety. We have a vivid picture of it, put sarcastically by the Christian poet Prudentius into the mouth of a martyr named Romanus:

> As you know, a trench is dug, and the high priest
> plunges deep underground to be sanctified.
> He wears a curious headband, fastens fillets for the occasion
> around his temples, fixes his hair with a crown of gold,
> holds up his robes of silk with a belt from Gabii.
> Over his head they lay a plank-platform criss-cross,
> fixed so that the wood is open not solid;
> then they cut or bore through the floor
> and make holes in the wood with an awl at several points
> till it is plentifully perforated with small openings.

A large bull, with grim, shaggy features
and garlands of flowers round his neck
or entangling his horns, is escorted to the spot.
The victim's head is shimmering with gold
and the sheen of the gold leaf lends colour to his hair.
The animal destined for sacrifice is at the appointed place.
They consecrate a spear and with it pierce his breast.
A gaping wound disgorges a stream of blood,
still hot, and pours a steaming flood on the lattice
of the bridge below, flowing copiously.
Then the shower drops through the numerous paths offered
by the thousand cracks raining a ghastly dew.
The priest in the pit below catches the drops,
puts his head underneath each one till it is stained,
till his clothes and all his body are soaked in corruption.
Yes, and he lays his head back, puts his cheeks in the stream,
sets his ears underneath, gets lips and nose in the way,
bathes his very eyes in the drops
does not spare his mouth, wets his tongue
till he drains deep the blood with every pore.
When the blood is exhausted the priests drag away
the carcase, now growing stiff, from the structure of planks.
Then the high priest emerges, a grim spectacle.
He displays his dripping head, his congealed beard,
his sopping ornaments, his clothes inebriated.
He bears all the stains of this polluting rite,
filthy with the gore of the atoning victim just offered—
and everyone stands to one side, welcomes him, honours him,
just because he has been buried in a beastly pit
and washed with the wretched blood of a dead ox.

> Prudentius *Peristephanon* 10, 1011-50.

Many inscriptions record initiates who claim to be "reborn into eternal life by the baptisms in bull's and ram's blood."

Isis and her consort Osiris were Egyptian gods of great antiquity. Isis is in fact the land of Egypt, and Osiris the fertilizing waters of the Nile, but also the corn which comes from the interaction of land and river: "this is the form of him whom one may not name, Osiris of Mysteries, who springs from the returning waters." But in the Hellenistic and Roman periods Isis became a universal goddess who at one and the same time made universal claims and particular claims to be a unique saviour.

Among the earliest Greek documents relating to Isis are four hymns, written by one Isidorus (presumably his Isiac name), and found in the Fayum: they were probably written about 100 B.C. In this she is the universal goddess, with three main titles, Good Fortune, Demeter and Hermouthis. The first is perhaps the finest of the hymns.

> Giver of wealth, Queen of the gods, lady Hermouthis,
> ruler of all, Good Fortune, Isis of the great name,
> exalted Deo, Discoverer of all life,
> you put your hand to mighty works of all kinds, so as to give
> life and an ordered society to all mankind,
> you introduced laws so that there might be a measure of justice,
> you revealed sciences so that men might live decently,
> you discovered the flowering nature of all fruitful plants.
> For you the sky came into being, the whole earth,
> the breath of the breezes, the sun with its welcome radiance.
> By your power the streams of the Nile are all filled full
> at the summer season, and its water pours turbulent
> over the whole land so that the crop may never fail.
> All mortals who live on the limitless earth,
> Thracians, Greeks, and foreigners as well,
> utter your glorious name which all honour,
> each in his own language, each in his own land.
> Syrians call you Astarte, Artemis, Nanaea,
> the tribes of Lycia call you Queen Leto,
> men in Thrace call you Mother of the gods,
> Greeks call you Hera of the lofty throne, and Aphrodite,
> kindly Hestia, Rheia, and Demeter.
> Egyptians call you Thiouis because you, being One, are all
> the other goddesses named by all peoples.
> My Lady, I shall not stop hymning your mighty power,
> immortal Saviour, goddess of the many names, almighty Isis,
> rescuing from war cities and all their citizens,
> men, their wives, possessions and dear children.
> All who are held in the destiny of death, all in bondage,
> all who are racked with pain which will not let them sleep,
> all men journeying in a foreign country,
> all who sail on the great sea in stormy weather,
> when ships are wrecked and men lose their lives—
> all these find salvation if they pray for your present help.

Hear my prayers, you whose name has mighty power,
be propitious to me and free me from all affliction.

> V.F. Vanderlip *The Four Greek Hymns of Isidorus
> and the Cult of Isis.*

Other hymns by Isidorus show the goddess as prospering com-
merce, granting children, and blessing the sovereign, and speak of
her omnipresence from north to south and east to west, or riding in
the Sun's Chariot as the dispenser of justice.

Apuleius' racy novel *The Metamorphoses* or *The Golden Ass* was
written in the second half of the second century A.D. It turns out
that behind the collection of entertaining and often bawdy anecdotes is a serious religious purpose. Lucius, who has been turned
into a donkey, is saved by Isis, who makes all the universal claims
which we find in Isidorus' hymn and in other aretalogies. Lucius
resolves on initiation into the service of the goddess.

After this I became even more devoted in my attendance on the
goddess's service. I thought my present blessings gave promise
for the future. Every day my eagerness to take holy orders grew. I
was importunate in sharing this with the high priest, pressing to
be initiated into the mysteries of the holy night. He was a man of
solemn bearing, with a high reputation for dutiful religious observances. He treated me as parents treat children who have not
seen the full implications of their requests, gently dispelling my
importunity and calming my restlessness of spirit with the promise
of better things to come. He told me that the goddess would sig-
nify her approval of the day of initiation, would be careful to select
the priest to perform the ceremony, and would indicate how the
expenses of the ritual should be met. I should need remarkable
patience in waiting for all this to happen. I must avoid the extremes of overeagerness, leading to impatience before my calling,
and obstinacy, leading to hesitation in answering the call when it
came. To enter our Lady's service without her express command
would be temerarious, it would be sacrilegious, it would be invit-
ing destruction, it would be the sign of an abandoned, suicidal
character, and none of the brotherhood would have the effrontery
to behave in such a way. The keys of hell and the promise of life
were in the goddess's hands. The actual process of initiation led to
something like a voluntary death and a return to life which depended on her favour. When a man had fulfilled his span of life

and was standing at the very gates of nightfall, provided that he could keep safe the mighty mysteries of her cult, she could rescue him by her divinity, bring him to rebirth, and by her providence set him back on the path of new life. So I must wait for orders from above, even though I was clearly predestinated to her glorious ministry by supreme marks of her divine favour. Meanwhile, like her other worshippers I must abstain from eating forbidden food so that when the time came I could move directly into the pure depths of her religious mysteries.

I received the priest's advice, and did not allow impatience to mar my service. I took part daily in the temple services, concentrating gently, quietly, silently to earn her approval. The great goddess's kindness in salvation did not let me down or torture me with a long period of waiting. In the darkness of the night she gave me a clear injunction that the day I was always longing for had arrived, the day on which my supreme prayer would be granted. She told me how much I would need to spend on the ceremony, and that she was appointing her high priest Mithras in charge of the ritual; our horoscopes, she said, harmonized. These and the other welcome instructions from the Supreme Goddess stirred me to new life. Although dawn had not yet broken, I put sleep aside and went straight to find the high priest. I met him coming out of his room and was prompt to greet him. It had been my intention to claim initiation as my right with more than any normal urgency, but the moment he saw me, he got in first. "Lucius," he said, "you are richly blessed. The goddess in her majesty has freely bestowed her grace on you. Why are you standing doing nothing? Why this delay? The day you prayed for so earnestly has dawned, the day for your initiation at my hands into the most sacred mysteries at the express command of the Goddess of the Many Names."

The old man took me by the hand and led me courteously to the entrance of the colossal temple, and performed the ritual opening and the morning sacrifice. Then he produced from the temple treasury a number of books written in characters unknown to me, some of them animal hieroglyphics to convey ordinary language in summary form, others protected against the inquisitive tendencies of the uninitiated by being knotted together or twisted like a wheel or with their tops linked in a spiral pattern. From these books he produced oracular utterances about the preparations I must make for initiation. Without delay I set myself actively to deal with the purchase of the necessary material, personally or through my friends, sparing no expense. When the time demanded it (according to the priest) he escorted me in ceremonial procession to baths nearby.

There I went through the ritual cleansing. He asked the gods for
grace, purified me by aspersion, and took me back to the temple at
about two in the afternoon, positioning me at the very feet of the
goddess, and giving me privately certain instructions too sacred to
be spoken out loud, and publicly enjoining me to fast for ten consecutive days, abstaining completely from meat and wine. I religiously observed these precepts continently and respectfully.

Now at last the day fixed for my vows to the goddess was arriv-
ing. The sun began to sink and evening came on. Suddenly from
every direction came a flood of initiates offering me different gifts
according to ancient tradition. All the uninitiated were sent away.
The priest arrayed me in a fresh linen robe, took my hand, and led
me to the inner sanctuary of the shrine. I expect that if you are a
serious reader you are eager to learn all that I saw and heard. I
would tell you, if I were allowed to tell you and you were allowed
to hear—but your ears and my tongue would alike be punished for
such rash inquisitiveness. However, in case you are religiously inclined I have no desire to leave you in a long torment of suspense.
So listen and have faith. What I am telling you is the truth. I approached the frontiers of death. I set food in Proserpina's doorway. I was torn back through all the elements. At midnight I saw
the sun blazing with golden light. I approached the presence of
the gods below and the gods above, and worshipped them from
close at hand. There, I have told you. You have heard and must
disown it. I shall now confine myself to material which can be re-
lated to the understanding of the uninitiated without offence.

Morning came, and the ceremony was over. I emerged wearing twelve sacred stoles, a mystic apparel which I may nonetheless
speak of freely, seeing that plenty of people saw me at the time. I
was told to mount a wooden platform erected in the very heart of
the temple before the goddess's statue. I was wearing a vestment
of fine linen embroidered with flowers: a valuable cope was rest-
ing on my shoulders and reached down my back to my ankles.
Wherever you looked I was splendid with animals worked in different colours: snakes from India on one side, griffins from the far
north (a kind of winged flying creature generated in the other part
of the world) on the other. The priests call this "the stole of Olympus." In my hand I was carrying a lighted torch, and I was wearing
on my head a lovely garland, with white palm-leaves projecting in
every direction like the rays of the sun. Suddenly a curtain was
pulled aside, and the people flocked to see me, dressed as I was
like the sun and looking like a statue. Next I gave a party to celebrate my birthday in the religion; there was excellent food and
cheerful company. The next day but one was celebrated with a

similar ceremony, including a sacred breakfast which formally ended my initiation. But I remained in the same place for some days. I was taking an insatiable delight in the goddess's statue, naturally as she had bound me to her by a grace I could not requite. In the end at the goddess's own injunction I prepared to return home, reluctantly tearing myself from the harbour I loved so dearly. But first I paid a debt of gratitude, not in full, but as best I could. I prostrated myself before the goddess, I bathed her feet with the tears which sprang from my eyes, and with many a gulp cutting into my words I said:

"Holy goddess, everlasting Saviour of mankind, ever generous in your help to mortals, you show a mother's warm love for the misfortunes of those in distress. No day passes, no night, no moment however fleeting without a gracious act of yours. You protect human beings by sea and land. You lull the storms of life and stretch out your hand to rescue them. You can unravel the inextricably tangled web of Fate. You can calm the gales of Fortune. You can hold back the stars from baleful movements. The gods above worship you, the gods below honour you. You set the universe in motion, you give light to the sun, you govern the world, you trample Hell beneath your feet. The stars obey you, the seasons return at your bidding, the spiritual powers delight in you, the elements are your slaves. At your command the breezes blow, the clouds bring growth, seeds shoot and shoots ripen. Your majestic presence overawes the birds flocking in the sky, the wild animals roaming over the mountains, the snakes skulking the earth, the monsters swimming in the sea. My ability is too scanty to praise you properly, my resources too scanty to honour you with sacrifice. My eloquence is insufficient to say all I feel about your majesty—even had I a thousand mouths and a thousand tongues, and the power of speaking forever without wearying. But poor as I am I have taken a vow of devotion and shall be dutiful in doing all that I can. I shall always guard the picture of your divine features and your holy godhead in the secret places of my heart."

Apuleius *Metamorphoses* 11, 21-5.

Three things call for especial comment here. The first is that the initiation is a spiritual death and rebirth. The second is the appearance of the reborn initiate in an epiphany; he has become a visible manifestation of the sun-god. The third is the very real personal devotion: it is not too much to say that Lucius loves Isis.

Mithraism must be mentioned, though it was never quite as

important as some of its interpreters make out. It is found chiefly in ports and military bases, and the underground sanctuaries are usually quite small. It came from the East. Mithras was born of the rock, a saviour-god, who caught and killed the sacred bull whose life brought fertility to the earth. Mithras and his ally the Sun were generals in the war of Light against Darkness. Initiates were promised the support of Mithras when under judgement after death. Much of our knowledge comes from archaeology. It may be interesting to see a satirical attack on the cult by a rather bad Christian poet.

> If he is reckoned a god, invincible, born of the rock,
> Now I'll say nothing; do you assign priority between them.
> Vote the rock first, the god second, and search for the rock's creator.
> In addition to this you also portray a thief, although
> Crime is no way for a god to live at all.
> Totally earthy he is, unnatural in character
> Veering the cattle of others away in caves.
> So Vulcan's son Cacus used to behave in the past.
>
> Commodianus Instructions 1, 13.

> The verses are an acrostic on INVICTUS, "invincible." Commodianus in fact alludes to six important points about Mithras (a) his divine status (b) his title of "invincible" (c) his birth from the rock (d) the descent of the soul from the outer heavens in Mithraic thought (e) the killing of the sacred bull (f) the fact that the sacrificial act took place in a cave, and the chapels were called "caves." Cacus was a legendary cattle-thief.

There were seven grades of initiation. The Servitors were Raven, Bridegroom, Soldier; the Participants were Lion, Persian, Courier of the Sun, Father. Members wore appropriate costumes to their grade. Initiation at all points involved ordeals.

> Different people take different views of Mithras: some regard him as the Sun, others as the Guardian of Fire, others attribute to him some specific power. There are initiatory ceremonies for this Mithras, especially among the Chaldaeans. Those initiated are initiated through graded ordeals. First they experience lighter ordeals, then more severe ones. They begin by requiring the initiates to fast for perhaps fifty days. If they show courageous endurance

through this they require them to undergo two days laceration and then twenty days exposure to snow. In this way they gradually increase the ordeals, and if the initiate succeeds in enduring them, then for the future they account him a fully initiated member.

Nonnus the Mythographer 18.

The account may be exaggerated.

Tertullian gives an account of initiation into the grade of soldier.

Fellow-soldiers of Christ, you should be ashamed to take your standards not from Christ but from one of the soldiers of Mithras. They are initiated in a cave, in the very camp of darkness. A wreath is presented to them, hung on a sword—it is a kind of parody of martyrdom. It is prepared for their head, but they are advised to put up their hands and remove it from their heads, perhaps transferring it to their shoulder with the words "Mithras is my crown."

Tertullian *On the Wreath* 15.

Christianity entered the Graeco-Roman world as just such another mystery-religion.

The first Christian sermon was preached to Jews at Pentecost by Peter, and its presuppositions are those of Hellenistic Judaism.

". . . Men of Israel, listen to my words. Jesus of Nazareth was a man marked out by God before you by supernatural powers, portents and signs; which God performed through him in your presence, as you well know. He was handed over to you by God's determinate will and foreknowledge, and you used Gentiles to execute him by crucifixion. But God raised him to life again, freeing him from the birthpangs of death, since it was not possible for death to master him. For David says of him:

I foresaw that the Lord would be always with me,
since he is at my right hand to save me from collapse.
For this reason my heart was light and my tongue expressed its joy,
and my body will continue to lodge in hope.
For you will not abandon my soul to death

or allow one dedicated to you to see corruption.
You have made the paths of life clear to me;
you will fill me with joy as a result of your presence.

Brothers, I can say frankly to you that the patriarch David died and was buried; his tomb has survived here to the present day. He was a prophet; he knew that God had solemnly sworn to him that he would establish one of his own physical descendants on his throne. When he said that he was not abandoned to death, and that his soul did not see corruption he was speaking prophetically of the resurrection of the Messiah. It was this Jesus whom God raised from the dead, and we are all witnesses to the fact. He was raised high by God's hand, he received the promise of the Holy Spirit from the Father, and all that you see and hear flows from him. It was not David who made the ascent to heaven; as he puts it himself,

The Lord said to my Lord, Sit on my right,
so that I can turn your enemies into a footstool for your feet.

The whole family of Israel can know for sure that God has made this Jesus whom you crucified both Lord and the Messiah."

When they heard this they were cut to the heart, and said to Peter and the other apostles, "Brothers, what are we to do?" Peter replied, "Have a change of heart. Be baptized, all of you, in the name of Jesus the Messiah so that your sins may be forgiven, and you will receive the gift of the Holy Spirit. For the promise belongs to you and your children, and to all whom our Lord God calls in ages to come." He gave his testimony further at length, and spoke to them earnestly, saying, "Find salvation from this crooked generation." Those who accepted what he said were baptized, and some three thousand souls were enrolled on that very day. They gave themselves enthusiastically to the apostles' teaching, to the common life, to the breaking of the bread and to prayer.

Luke *Acts of Apostles* 2:22-42.

> The Messiah of Christ was God's Anointed servant who was expected to bring in the kingdom of God. We notice the initiatory ceremony of baptism, the promise of forgiven sin and divine inspiration, and the shared life of the initiates, as well as the theme of resurrection.

One saying of Jesus comes very close to the words and thought of Eleusis.

The hour has come for the Son of Man to be glorified. Yes, yes—I tell you, if a grain of wheat does not fall into the ground and die it remains single. If it dies, it bears much fruit. The man who loves his self loses it. The man who hates his self in this world will preserve it for eternal life.

John 12:23-25.

> The Son of Man is a difficult phrase. In one sense a son of man is simply a human being. But the phrase was applied to a symbolic being appearing in eschatological visions. It was not inescapably a Messianic title. It has been argued that Jesus used it as a single figure denoting the new community of himself and his followers, though at the last he was left alone. The word translated "self" is *psyche*, often rendered "soul," here with a strong implication of "life."

Christianity began to spread outside the bounds of Judaism largely through the instrumency of one man, Paul of Tarsus: his Jewish name was Saul, but as he moved out into the Gentile world he increasingly used his Roman name. How far his thinking was influenced by the Hellenistic mystery-religions is controversial, but he certainly was not afraid to use their language.

See, I am telling you a mystery. We shall not all sleep, but we shall all be changed in an instant, in the twinkling of an eye, at the final trumpet. The trumpet will sound, the dead will be raised free from corruption, and we shall be changed! This being which is subject to corruption must put on incorruptible robes, this our mortal being must don immortality. Then the scripture shall be fulfilled which says "Death is swallowed up: the result is victory." Death, where is your victory? Death, where is your power to goad us? Death's goad is sin. Sin's power lies in the Law. But, praise God! He gives us victory through our Lord Jesus the Messiah.

Paul I *Corinthians* 15:51-57.

> Here the promise is of life beyond death; it is linked with the conquest of sin; the victory for the Christian depends on Jesus, as it does for the Isiac on Isis and for the Mithraist on Mithras.

Christian writers attack the other mystery-religions, but partly because they see them as a devil's parody on their own beliefs and practices. In their attacks they give some important information, often tantalizing, about the content of the Mysteries.

The mysteries are simply tradition and idle invention; it is worshipping one of the devil's tricks when people honour with bas-
tard religiosity these unholy holinesses and impious initiations.
Think of the mystic chests—I am bound to strip the veil from their
sacred rites and shout aloud their mystic secrets. What is in them
but sesame-cakes, triangular cakes, round cakes, cakes shaped
with hollows like navels, balls of salt, and a snake, symbol of
Dionysus Bassareus? And pomegranates besides, and boughs of
fig, and fennel, and ivy, yes and biscuits and poppies? These are
their holy things! And what of the symbols of Ge Themis, which
no one is supposed to reveal—marjoram, a lamp, a sword, a woman's "comb" (a religious euphemism for a woman's sex-organ).
It's downright shamelessness! There was a time when for men of
self-control night was a silent cover for their pleasures. Now for
these initiates night is a time for open talk, a temptation to misbe-
haviour, and the flame of the torches reveals and convicts their
lusts. Put out the flame, priest. Have some shame for the torch,
acolyte. The light convicts this Iacchus of yours. Let night cover
your mysteries, and the ceremonies be shown the darkness they
deserve. The fire is not acting a part: judgement and execution are
its function.

Clement of Alexandria
Exhortation to the Greeks 2.

The early years of the Christian era saw the rise of Gnosticism.
The Gnostics were a heterogeneous group who promised revealed
knowledge (*gnosis*) as the condition of escape from the world of
matter into the world of spirit. They were generally dualists, and
offered a complex cosmogony and scheme of salvation. One of the
finest specimens of Gnostic literature is "The Hymn of the Pearl"
incorporated into the apocryphal *Acts of Thomas*.

When I was a small child,
    living in my Father's royal palace,
delighting in the rich luxury
    of those who brought me up,
my parents sent me away from our home
    in the East with provisions for the journey,
fixing me with a pack
    filled from the wealth of their treasury,
bulky but light,
    for me to carry without help—

gold from the land of Ellaea,
  silver of great Gazzak,
rubies from India,
  pearls from Kushan.
They armed me with adamant
  which can smash iron.
They took off me the glorious robe
  which they had made me in their love,
and the purple cloak
  woven to my size.
They made an agreement with me
  and wrote it on my heart for remembrance:
"If you go down into Egypt
  and fetch back the single pearl
which lies in the middle of the sea,
  encircled by a hissing snake,
then you shall again put on your glorious robe
  and your cloak over it,
and become heir to our kingdoms
  along with the next in line, your brother."
I left the East and travelled down
  with two attendants,
for the road was dangerous and difficult
  and I was young for such a journey.
I passed the borders of Maishan
  where the merchants of the East gather;
I came to the land of Babel
  and entered the walls of Sarbug.
When I reached Egypt,
  my attendants left me.
I made straight for the snake
  and took up lodging close to his nest,
waiting for him to slumber and sleep
  so that I could take my pearl from him.
I was alone and on my own,
  a stranger to the others there.
Yet I saw there one of my own people,
  a freeborn man from the East,
a pleasant attractive lad,
  son of anointed kings.
. . . .
  he came and attached himself to me.
I made friends with him,
  and shared my mission with him.

He warned me against the Egyptians
  and contact with unclean people.
I put on clothes like theirs
  for fear that they should spot me as a foreigner
come to take the pearl,
  and arouse the snake against me.
But somehow or other
  they discovered I was not of their country.
So they plotted a cunning ruse,
  giving me their food to eat,
and I forgot that I was a king's son,
  and enlisted with their king,
and forgot the pearl
  for which my parents had sent me.
Through the heaviness of their food
  I fell into a deep sleep.
My parents saw all that happened to me
  and were distressed for me.
They made a proclamation throughout our kingdom
  that all should gather at our gates.
The kings and rulers of Parthia
  and all the nobility of the East
debated how to save me
  from being left in Egypt.
They wrote me a letter
  signed by all the nobility:
"From the king of kings, your Father,
  and the Queen of the East, your Mother,
and your brother, the next in rank,
  to our son in Egypt, greetings.
Wake up! Arise from sleep!
  Attend to the words of our letter!
Remember you are a son of kings!
  Look at your present slave's state!
Remember the pearl
  for which you made the journey to Egypt!
Remember your glorious robe
  and the splendid cloak,
which you are to put on to adorn you,
  when your name is in the book of heroes
and you are to be heir to our kingdom
  with your brother, our vice-regent."
Mine was a letter
  sealed with the king's own hand

against the wicked sons of Babel
    and the violent demons of Sarbug.
It took wings in the form of an eagle,
    the king of all birds,
flying till it alighted by me,
    and turned back to words.
At its voice and noise
    I started up out of sleep.
I picked it up, kissed it,
    broke the seal, and read.
The words of the letter matched
    what was written in my heart.
I remembered that I was a son of kings
    and my free nature longed for its fellows.
I remembered the pearl
    for which I had been sent down to Egypt.
Then I set myself to enchant
    the terrible hissing snake.
I charmed him to sleep
    by speaking my Father's name over him,
the name of the next in line
    and of the Queen of the East, my Mother.
I seized the pearl.
    I started back to my Father's house.
I took off their impure, filthy clothes,
    and left them in their country.
I made straight
    for the light of our Eastern homeland.
On the road in front I found
    the letter which had aroused me.
Just as its voice had aroused me,
    now its light guided me.
The royal robe of silk
    shone before my eyes
and with its voice and guidance
    encouraged me to hurry,
led me with its love,
    drew me forward.
I passed by Sarbug,
    leaving Babel on the left,
and reached great Maishan,
    the harbour of merchants,
that is situated
    on the shore of the sea.

The glorious robe which I had taken off
    and the cloak I had once worn
had been sent by my parents
    from the heights of Hyrcania
by the hand of their treasurers,
    men to whom it could be entrusted.
I had forgotten its beauty,
    having left it in my Father's palace when a boy.
Suddenly as I looked at it,
    I seemed to be seeing myself in a mirror.
I saw it complete in myself,
    I saw myself complete in it.
We were divided into two,
    but one in form.
I saw also the treasurers
    who brought me the robe,
two in number, one in form,
    one royal mark on both.
They were carrying my treasure
    and restored it in full,
with my glorious robe
    colourfully ornamented
with gold and beryls,
    rubies and agates,
and sardonyx of many hues,
    ready for its home above,
and all its seams fixed
    with stones of adamant,
and the image of the king of kings
    depicted all over it,
and its variegated colours
    gleaming like sapphire.
I saw shimmering through it
    the movements of knowledge.
I saw it preparing
    to utter words.
I heard the tones
    it murmured as it came down:
"I am one with the valiant hero,
    brought up for him in my Father's house.
I sensed in myself
    my stature growing with his acts."
With royal movements
    it spread towards me,

reaching out for me to take it
    from the hands of those who brought it;
and my love drove me
    to run to it and hold it.
I reached out and took it
    and decked myself in its brilliant colours,
and wrapped all round me
    my royal cloak.
Wearing these I went up
    to the place of greeting and homage.
I bowed my head and paid homage
    to the majesty of my Father who sent it.
I had fulfilled his orders;
    he had fulfilled his promises.
I mixed with his nobles
    at his palace-gates.
He welcomed me with you,
    and I was with him in his kingdom,
and all his servants praised him
    in musical tones.
He promised me to travel with him
    to the court of the king of kings,
and with the gift of the pearl
    to appear with him before the King.

R.A. Lipsius and M. Bonnet
Acta Apostolorum Apocrypha 112 pp 214 ff
A.A. Bevan *Texts and Studies* V 3.

The text, no doubt originally in Syriac, is found both in Syriac and Greek. As I have no Syriac I have had to rely on other interpreters for the meaning of that text. Some verses are quite uncertain. The Father's house in the East from which the Son comes down is clearly the heavenly home, and Egypt with its filthy clothes is the material world. The snake is a symbol of the powers of darkness, and the waters are the darkness of the material world. The robe seems to be the true self, preserved in heaven. But there are some ambiguities in the story. The pearl is on the face of it the soul. But although the Son should be the Saviour, he too is drugged by the material world and forgets his mission, and this does not accord with his being the Saviour. Rather do the Son and his journey seem to be an allegory of the human soul in its descent into matter and return to its heavenly home, the letter being the revelation of Gnosis or knowledge. But then what is the pearl? Perhaps Hans Jonas' suggestion is right. The pearl *is* the soul, and the Son is Primal Man, the pre-cosmic divinity who is sent to recover what is his own, and yet is also present in the darkness of every human soul.

Another sect offering salvation through rebirth to its initiates was found in Egypt during the first three centuries A.D. and associated with the divine figure of Hermes the Thrice-Greatest who is also the Egyptian Thoth. The documents do in fact show a strange amalgam of Egyptian, Greek and oriental approaches. The first, called *Poimandres* or *The Shepherd of Mankind*, ends with a magnificent prayer.

> Holy is the God and Father of all, existing before the world began.
> Holy is God, whose will is fulfilled by his own powers.
> Holy is God, who wills to be known and is known by those who
>   are his.
>   Holy are you, who by your Word fashioned all that exists.
>   Holy are you, who cannot be darkened by the world of matter.
>   Holy are you, and all nature is your image.
>   Holy are you, and stronger than all dominion.
>   Holy are you, and greater than all that is greatest.
>   Holy are you, and beyond all praise.
> You who are ineffable, inexpressible, utterable only in silence,
>   receive
>   these sacred offerings of words from a soul and heart which
>   reaches up to you.
> Grant my prayer that I may never fall away from the knowledge
>   which
>   accords with our inmost being. Fill me with power so that in
>   receiving your grace I may enlighten those of my race who are
>   in ignorance, my brothers, your children.
> For this reason I have faith and testify that I am entering into life
>   and light.
> Blessed are you, Father. The man who is yours wishes to share your
>   holiness, as you have bestowed on him all authority.
>   *Corpus Hermeticum* 1 *(Poimandres)* 31-2.

The other particularly important tractate is the thirteenth, sometimes called *The Secret Discourse on the Mountain*.

> "Father, in your general account, when you were discussing divinity, you spoke allusively rather than openly. You said that no one can be saved until he has been born again, but you did not reveal for all my questions what this means. After your words to me I begged to learn the doctrine of rebirth, since that is the only

doctrine I do not understand, but you did not think it wise yet to convey it to me and said 'When you are ready to separate yourself from the world, then I will share it with you'. I am now so ready. I have kept my thought separate from the world's illusions. So make good my deficiencies, as you promised when you put before me the prospect that you would teach me about rebirth. Thrice-greatest, I do not understand from what womb or seed a man can be born again." "My son, the womb is Wisdom, conceiving in silence, and the seed the True Good." "Who is it, father, who provides the seed? I am utterly at a loss." "The Will of God, my son." "Tell me this as well. Who is the midwife who brings rebirth to fruition?" "Some man, who is a son of God and subjects himself to God's will." "What sort of man is it, father, who experiences birth?" "The man who is so born is changed, a son of God, a God himself, All, and in all, without any share of corporeality, but sharing in incorporeal being, being formed entirely of divine potency." "Father, you're talking in riddles, not as father to son."

"Son, this sort of thing cannot be taught; God recalls it to our minds when he will." "Father, what you say is impossible; your language is forced. I am fully justified in asking in reply 'Am I a cuckoo in the nest?' Father, don't be so grudging; I am your true son. Explain to me fully the nature of this rebirth." "What am I to say, my son? This is not a thing which can be taught. It is not possible to see it with the physical constitution of the eyes. All I can say is this. I see that by the mercy of God there has come into being within me an immaterial form, and I have passed into an immortal body. I am not now as I was before: I have experienced spiritual rebirth, and my previous form has been dissolved. I am no longer coloured, tangible, three-dimensional. I am now a stranger to all that, and a stranger to all that you discern through the medium of physical eyesight. I am now not visible to eyes of that kind, my son." "Father, you've driven me completely, frantically out of my wits. At this moment do my eyes not see myself." "I could wish, my son, that you too had passed out of yourself, so that you could see not like men dreaming in their sleep, but wide awake."

"Father, I'm at a loss for words. I can see you, father, your stature just as it was, with the same familiar features." "Even here you're wrong. Our mortal form changes day by day. As time passes it becomes larger or smaller. It is in fact an illusion." "Where then is truth, Thrice-greatest?" "In that which is not polluted, my son, not bounded, colourless, formless, without qualities, brilliant, that which is apprehended by itself alone, unchanging, immutable, the Good." "I really am crazy, father; I've lost what sense I had. I thought I'd received the gift of wisdom at your hands, but when you lay this thought in front of me my powers of perception are stopped up." "Quite right, my son. The elements which rise and sink, which are liquid or serve our breathing, are the objects of sense-perception. How do you imagine you can perceive with the senses something quite different from these, not solid or liquid, not firmly bound, not easily dissolved, apprehensible only by divine power and requiring the power of spiritual apprehension?" "Don't I possess that power, father?" "Heaven forbid that you should not, my son. Draw it into yourself, and it will come; wish for it, and it comes true. Control the activities of your physical senses and divinity will be born within you. But you must purify yourself from the irrational torments of matter." "Have I really torturers inside myself, father?" "Yes, my son, and plenty of them, and terrifying they are." "Father, I don't understand."

"This ignorance of yours is one of the tortures, my son. The second is distress, the third incontinence, the fourth lust, the fifth injustice, the sixth ambition, the seventh error, the eighth jealousy, the ninth mischief-making, the tenth anger, the eleventh impetuosity, the twelfth vice. There are these, twelve in number, and under them many more, my son. They use the senses to compel the man who is incarcerated in the prison of the body to suffer torments. But they leave a man in a pack when God shows mercy on him, and in this way his rational faculty is built up. That is what I mean by rebirth. And now, my son, keep a solemn silence; so God's mercies will not fail us. Now my son, be happy; the powers of God are in the process of purifying you; they are here to build up your rational faculty. The knowledge of God has come upon us, and with her arrival, son, ignorance has been banished. Happiness has come, and in her presence, my son, distress will escape to those who have room for her. After happiness I next invoke continence. Loveliest of powers! Son, let us give her a warm welcome. At the moment of her arrival she has pushed out incontinence. Fourth I invoke self-discipline, the power opposed to lust. This platform, son, is the seat of justice; see how she has expelled injustice. In the absence of injustice, my son, we have received acquittal without a formal trial. The sixth power I invoke stands against ambition. She is a sense of community. One ambition has been driven away. . . . Seventh I invoke truth. Off with you, error; truth is here. See, son, how the presence of truth makes the Good complete: jealousy and the other torments have vanished. The Good follows hard on the heels of truth, accompanied by life and light. None of the torments of darkness assail us any longer; they have taken wings and rushed away. In this way, son, spiritual being has been made complete, and in its birth we have become gods. Anyone who through mercy receives this divine birth is freed from his physical senses, recognizes that he is formed of powers of God, and is glad in the knowledge." "Father, I realize that God has made of me a new being, realize it not with the sight of the eyes but with the operation of spiritual intelligence." "This is rebirth, my son, the perception not of three-dimensional matter but of immaterial being." "Father, with the eyes of spiritual intelligence, I see myself to be the Universe. I am in heaven, on earth, in water, in air. I am in animals and plants. I am a babe in the womb, a babe before conception, a babe after birth. I am everywhere." "Son, you have learned the nature of rebirth."

Corpus Hermeticum 13, 1-11.

The text is difficult and uncertain. I have followed W. Scott's *Hermetica* (Oxford 1924). Even so there are gaps, and some passages, notably the list of torments and the corresponding powers of God, may not belong to the original tractate, though they belong to the same framework of thought. The tractate, like some of the others, is a dialogue between Hermes the Thrice-Greatest and his son Tat. Its substance is clear. It is an exposition of spiritual rebirth, one of the mysteries of the Hermetic sect. We notice strong Platonism, in the doctrine of recollection, and the emphasis on the *immaterial*. There is also apparently (though this is controversial) some Christian influence. "The elements which rise and sink, are liquid or help our breathing" are of course fire, earth, water and air. The strong moralism is notable. The mystery-religions laid stern demands on their initiates. The last part of the passage cited takes us into the higher flights of mysticism, and may be paralleled from Hinduism, Buddhism, Islam, Christianity, and indeed some of the Nature-mystics. *Tat tvam asi*, "That art Thou."

The doctrine of salvation for initiates only is not an easy one for all to accept. Plutarch in his essay "How to Study Poetry" has a couple of anecdotes showing the problem the non-mystic has in accepting mystical claims.

We can employ Diogenes as advocate against Sophocles as well. Sophocles has stunned thousands of people into despair with his words about the mystery-religions:

Thrice-blest
are those mortals who see these mysteries
before reaching Death. For them alone beyond
lies life, for all others woe on woe.

Diogenes hearing something of the sort cried "What's that? Do you mean that a criminal like Pataecion will have a better destiny after death than Epaminondas just because he has been initiated?" Another story tells how Timotheus in the theatre was singing of Artemis as

> ecstatic Bacchic frantic fanatic

and Cinesias promptly shouted back, "I hope you have a daughter like that."

Plutarch *Moralia* 21F-22A.

(I have borrowed F.C. Babbitt's version of the assonant Greek of Timotheus' song.) The Sophocles passage is *fr.* 753. Diogenes' comment is not quite just, as the mystery-religions did require moral as well as ritual purity.

Still, pride in initiation remained, and we may fittingly end with an inscription which speaks of this.

To the Divine Shades. Vettius Agorius Praetextatus, Augur, Priest of Vesta, Priest of the Sun, Member of the Fifteen, Curial of Hercules, Consecrated to Liber and the deities of Eleusis, Hierophant, Superintendent Minister, initiated by the bull's blood Father of Fathers. In politics indeed Quaestor by special nomination, Praetor of the City, Governor of Tuscia and Umbria, Consular of Lusitania, Proconsul of Achaea, City Prefect, Appointed Ambassador by the Senate five times, twice Prefect of the Praetorian Guard in Italy and Illyrium, Nominated Consul Regular.

Also Aconia Fabia Paulina, daughter of Caius, Consecrated to Ceres and the Deities of Eleusis, Consecrated to Hecate on Aegina, initiated by the bull's blood, Hierophant.

These lived united together for forty years.

Ancestral glory gave me no greater blessing
than to be worthy of your hand.
My husband's name was all my light, my glory;
Agorius, born of a proud seed,
you brighten your country, your senate, your wife
by your integrity, character and learning,
which won you the crown of virtue.
All that wise men with heaven's gate open before them
have carefully handed down in Greek or Latin,
all that their learning embodied in verse,

all that they expressed in loose prose phrases,
all this you enhanced between reacting and recounting.
These are trifles. You are a pious initiate of the holy
mysteries and keep their revelations in the depth of your mind;
you have learned to honour the various gods in different ways,
and generously took your wife as partner in religion,
sharing your knowledge of gods and men, loyal to you.
Why should I now speak of your offices and titles,
the privileges men seek so earnestly.
You always thought them minor, fleeting;
your highest honour was the priestly fillet.
My husband, you took me, instructed me in the good,
kept me pure and holy, snatched me from the grasp of death,
brought me to the temples, dedicated me to serve the gods;
you were my sponsor as I entered the mysteries;
when I became priestess of Cybele and Attis,
you, my true partner, honoured me with the mystic blood of bulls;
when I became a servant of Hecate you taught me the triple secret;
you presented me as a worthy initiate of Ceres at Eleusis.
It is through you that all men honour me
devout and blest, for you spread my good name
through all the world. Unknown myself, I am known to all.
How should men not honour your wife?
The mothers of Rome treat me as an example,
and think their children lovely if like you.
Men and women alike welcome and look to
the glories you have taught them to wear.
These are gone. I, your wife, am racked with tears,
blessed indeed, if the god had granted my husband
longer life than myself, but blessed even so
because I am, have been, and after death shall be yours.

CIL 6, 1, 1779.

From other sources we know that Vettius Agorius Praetextatus was proconsul of Achaea in 361 or 362, city prefect from 366 to 368, an ambassador in A.D. 368, and praetorian prefect in 384, dying the following year. Jerome calls him a sacrilegious idolater, but Macrobius several times praises his religious knowledge and devotion.

INDEX OF PASSAGES CITED

Periodicals

CLASSICAL

Acta Classica, c/o Miss L. Baumback, The University, Cape Town, Republic of South Africa

American Classical Review, Professor Ursula Schoenheim, Queens College, CUNY, Flushing, NY 11367, U.S.A.

American Journal of Philology, Professor H.T. Rowell, Johns Hopkins University, Baltimore, MD, U.S.A.

Atene e Roma, Casa Editrice Felice le Monnier, Via Scipione Ammirato 100, 50156 Firenze, Italy

Athenaeum, Università, Pavia, Italy

Classical Bulletin, Department of Classics, St. Louis University, St. Louis, Missouri 63103, U.S.A.

Classical Journal, H. Jones Shey, Department of Classics, University of Wisconsin, Milwaukee, WI 53201, U.S.A.

Classical Philology, The Editor, Box 1, Faculty Exchange, University of Chicago, Ill. 60637, U.S.A.

Classical Review, c/o Clarendon Press, Oxford, England, U.K.

Classical World, 246 Maginnes Hall, Lehigh University, Bethlehem, PA 18015, U.S.A.

Greece and Rome, Clarendon Press, Oxford, England, U.K.

Hermathena, Professor E.J. Furlong, Trinity College, Dublin 2, Ireland

Journal of Hellenic Studies, The Librarian, 3104 Gordon Square, London WC1H OPD, England, U.K.

Latomus, M. Marcel Renard, Place Marie-Jose 13, 1050 Bruxelles, Belgium

Mnemosyne (Bibliotheca classica batava), E.J. Brill, Oude Rijn 33a-35, Leiden, Netherlands

Museum Africum, Department of Classics, University of Ibadan, Ibadan, Nigeria

Museum Helveticum, Schwabe and Co. Verlag, Basel 10, Switzerland

P.A.C.A., Department of Classics, University College, PH 167 H, Salisbury, Rhodesia

Phoenix, Trinity College, Toronto, Canada

Revue des Etudes Anciennes, M. Jacques Coupry, 29 Cours Pasteur, Bordeaux, France

Revue des Etudes Grecques, Les Belles Lettres, 95 Boulevard Raspail, Paris 6^e, France

POLITICAL AND GENERAL

Cambridge Review, c/o W. Heffer and Son Ltd., Trinity, Cambridge, England, U.K.

The Daily Telegraph, 135 Fleet Street, London EC4, England U.K.

Durham University Journal, c/o North Bailey, Durham DH1 3EX, England, U.K.

Eagle, St. John's College, Cambridge, England, U.K.

The Guardian, 2 Cross Street, Manchester, England, U.K.

Guardian Weekly, 164 Deansgate, Manchester M60 2RR, England, U.K.

New Statesman, 10 Great Turnstile, London WC1, England, U.K.

New World, c/o UNA, 93 Albert Embankment, London SE1 7TX, England, U.K.

The Observer, 160 Queen Victoria Street, London EC4V 4DA, England, U.K.

Open House, Open University, Walton Hall, Milton Keynes, MK7 6AA, England, U.K.

Peace News, 5 Caledonian Road, London N1, England, U.K.

Sesame, Open University, Walton Hall, Milton Keynes, MK7 6AA, England, U.K.

Spectator, 99 Gower Street, London WC1, England, U.K.

Stortfordian, Bishop's Stortford College, Bishop's Stortford, CM23 2QZ, Herts, England, U.K.

Sunday Telegraph, 135 Fleet Street, London EC4, England, U.K.

The Sunday Times, Thomson House, 200 Grays Inn Road, London EC4, England, U.K.

The Times, New Printing House Square, Grays Inn Road, London EC4, England, U.K.

Times Educational Supplement, Grays Inn Road, London EC4, England, U.K.

Times Higher Educational Supplement, Grays Inn Road, London EC4, England, U.K.

Times Literary Supplement, Grays Inn Road, London EC4, England, U.K.

RELIGIOUS

Baptist Quarterly, Rev. Dr. B. White, Regent's Park College, Oxford, England, U.K.

Christian Century, Christian Century Foundation, 407 S. Dearborn Street, Chicago, Ill. 60605, U.S.A.

Church Times, 7 Portugal Street, Kingsway, London WC2A 2HP, England, U.K.

Clarity, Jennifer Sprague, 3 Greenway, Berkhampsted, Herts, England, U.K.

Dawn, 331 Ormean Road, Belfast 7, Northern Ireland

Faith and Freedom, Bank Street Chapel Vestry, Crown Street, Bolton 3L1 2RU, England, U.K.

Fellowship, 523 North Broadway, Nyack, NY 10960, U.S.A.

The Friend, Drayton House, 30 Gordon Street, London WC1H OBQ, England, U.K.

The Heythrop Journal, Heythrop College, London, England, U.K.

Journal of Ecclesiastical History, Rev. Professor C.W. Dugmore, King's College, Strand, London WC2R 2LS, England, U.K.

Journal of Religion, University of Chicago, 1025 East 58th Street, Chicago, Ill. 60637, U.S.A.

Journal of Theological Studies, c/o Clarendon Press, Oxford, England, U.K.

Mennonite Quarterly Review, John S. Oyer, Goshen College, Goshen, Indiana 45626, U.S.A.

Methodist Recorder, 176 Fleet Street, London EC4A 2EP, England, U.K.

The Modern Churchman, Rev. H.C. Snape, The Corner House, Bampton, Oxford, England, U.K.

The Modern Free Churchman, Rev. D.G. Wigmore-Beddoes, 26 Cadogan Park, Belfast BT9 6HH, Northern Ireland

Movement, SCM Publications, 14 Prince Arthur Terrace, Rathmines, Dublin 6, Ireland

Nederlands Theologisch Tijdschrift, Dr. I.H. Enklaar, Terweeweg 9, Oestgeest, Netherlands

Newspeace, c/o Fellowship of Reconciliation, 9 Coombe Road, New Malden, Surrey KT 34QA, England, U.K.

Reconciliation Quarterly, c/o Fellowship of Reconciliation, 9 Coombe Road, New Malden, Surrey KT 3 4QA, England, U.K.

Religious Studies, Professor H.D. Lewis, King's College, Strand, London WC1R 2LS, England, U.K.

Scottish Journal of Theology, Rev. Professor T.F. Torrance, 37 Braid Farm Road, Edinburgh EH 10 6LE, Scotland, U.K.

Sojourners, 1029 Vermont Avenue NW, Washington, DC 20005, U.S.A.

Theology Today, Box 29, Princeton, NJ 08540, U.S.A.

Vision One, c/o BBC, 10 Eaton Gate, London SW1W 9BT, England, U.K.

World Faiths, Younghusband House, 23 Norfolk Square, London W2 1RU, England, U.K.

GENERAL INDEX

Entries in the Index of Passages are not repeated here.